# Classroom Instruction
## *that* Works

### 2nd Edition

CERI B. DEAN

ELIZABETH ROSS HUBBELL

HOWARD PITLER

Bj STONE

# Classroom Instruction
## *that* Works

RESEARCH-BASED STRATEGIES FOR INCREASING STUDENT ACHIEVEMENT

## 2nd Edition

ASCD
Alexandria, Virginia USA

MREL
Mid-continent Research for Education and Learning
Denver, Colorado USA

Boston   Columbus   Indianapolis   New York   San Francisco   Upper Saddle River
Amsterdam   Cape Town   Dubai   London   Madrid   Milan   Munich   Paris   Montreal   Toronto
Delhi   Mexico City   São Paulo   Sydney   Hong Kong   Seoul   Singapore   Taipei   Tokyo

1703 N. Beauregard St. • Alexandria, VA 22311-1714 USA
Phone: 800-933-2723 or 703-578-9600 • Fax: 703-575-5400
Website: www.ascd.org • E-mail: member@ascd.org
Author guidelines: www.ascd.org/write

### MᴄREL®

Mid-continent Research for Education and Learning
4601 DTC Boulevard, Suite 500
Denver, CO 80237 USA
Phone: 303-337-0990 • Fax: 303-337-3005
Website: www.mcrel.org • E-mail: info@mcrel.org

**This special edition published by Pearson Education, Inc. by arrangement with ASCD.**

Vice President and Editorial Director: Jeffery W. Johnston
Vice President and Publisher: Kevin Davis
Editorial Assistant: Lauren Carlson
Vice President, Director of Marketing: Margaret Waples
Senior Marketing Manager: Joanna Sabella
Senior Managing Editor: Pamela D. Bennett
Senior Operations Supervisor: Matt Ottenweller
Senior Art Director: Diane Lorenzo
Printer/Binder: Edwards Brothers Malloy
Cover Printer: Lehigh Press

**Library of Congress Cataloging-in-Publication Data**

Classroom instruction that works : research-based strategies for increasing student achievement / Ceri B. Dean ... [et al.]. -- 2nd ed.
    p. cm.
 Prev ed. cataloged under Marzano, Robert J.
 Includes bibliographical references and index.
 ISBN 978-1-4166-1362-6 (pbk. : alk. paper)
 1. Effective teaching--United States. 2. Academic achievement--United States--Statistics. I. Dean, Ceri B. II. Marzano, Robert J. Classroom instruction that works.
 LB1025.3.M339 2012
 371.102--dc23
           2011038223

10 9 8 7 6 5 4 3 2 1
ISBN 10:    0-13-336672-3
ISBN 13: 978-0-13-336672-3

# Classroom Instruction *that Works*

RESEARCH-BASED STRATEGIES
FOR INCREASING STUDENT ACHIEVEMENT

2nd Edition

Graphic organizers and bonus online-only content are available at www.ascd.org/citw.

Although there are many outcomes educators wish to influence in schools, achievement is certainly among the most critical. Too often, however, teachers and administrators focus on ensuring that all students reach standard benchmarks of performance, and much less attention is given to more critical aspects of progress. The fundamental obligation of education is to at least ensure that all students are making appropriate gains relative to the time they spend in classrooms. Of course, guaranteeing both—proficiency and progress—is ideal, but this book is concerned with helping those with a personal stake in education better understand the factors that lead to maximum gains.

One of the key features of this book is that it is based on a conceptual model that integrates the various "bits" of teaching and learning. This allows the authors to focus on showing how and why various strategies work more effectively than others. The answer, of course, is not identifying one method and adopting that new technique; rather, it is more about developing a wider worldview, or model, of how different influences in the classroom must work together to help all students realize their learning gains. The message here is that the nine categories of instruction presented in *Classroom Instruction That Works* are a powerful way of thinking about teaching and learning. This book highlights these instructional strategies rather than the different methods that may or may not use these strategies to various degrees. Having the flexibility to decide when and with whom to use the best strategy or mix of strategies is critical.

The "notable nine," therefore, can be powerfully invoked by teachers who wish to make a difference. For too long, educators were obsessed with models of *teaching*, preferring one method over another, rather than with models of *learning*. This book reminds us that we need to go back to models of learning and use them to help students see similarities and differences, learn how to summarize and take notes, practice deliberately, use imagery to build a deeper conceptual understanding on which they can "hang" surface level knowledge, learn from one another, solve problems, generate and test hypotheses, and give and receive feedback. Perhaps it is time to review our personal (and cultural) beliefs about teaching and see if the above strategies are well represented. If they are not, then why are they not? Let's pause and consider why such powerful strategies are not dominant in our instructional approach or in our thinking about how students learn.

A highlight of this second edition is the inclusion of relevant studies conducted during the past ten years—thus updating the previous edition of the book in a powerful way. The world has not stood still. We learned a lot in the intervening decade, and the order in which the authors present the strategies has changed to better reflect the current educational climate and a comprehensive framework that is geared toward instructional planning. I encourage you to read on and see what classroom instruction the evidence indicates works best.

—John Hattie

# Acknowledgments

This book builds on the work of Robert Marzano, Debra Pickering, and Jane Pollock, the authors of the first edition of *Classroom Instruction That Works*. There are many others who have contributed to this second edition whose names do not appear on the cover. They are the people from whom we drew inspiration and support. We thank McREL's talented research team—Andrea Beesley, Helen Apthorp, Charles Igel, Trudy Clemons Cherasaro, Jessica Allen, Tedra Clark, Sarah Gopalani, and Susie Bachler—who conducted the update of the meta-analysis and wrote the technical report from which this book draws information. Linda Brannan and Maura McGrath assisted with securing permissions and went beyond the call of duty to help us locate articles, books, and other resources to assist with the task. Mary Cullen and Wanda Garcia provided administrative assistance, helping us with the countless details that go with preparing a manuscript and keeping us calm when the seas were rough. Thanks also to our colleagues at McREL who encouraged us in countless ways and shared their experiences helping teachers use the strategies in *Classroom Instruction That Works*. We appreciate the financial support provided for this project by McREL's Management Council and the moral support provided by Tim Waters and David Frost.

We are grateful for the guidance and helpful comments provided by Nancy Modrak, Carolyn Pool, Scott Willis, and Jamie Greene of ASCD. Our reviewers, Henry Thiele, Matt Kuhn, Bryan Goodwin, and two anonymous others selected by ASCD, provided suggestions that helped us clarify our thinking and make improvements to our original draft. Equally important were their kind words of encouragement. We thank John Hattie for writing the foreword and for inspiring us with his work in general and his book *Visible Learning* in particular.

This book reflects our experience sharing information about the nine categories of instructional strategies with thousands of teachers and administrators across the United States and in several foreign countries over the last decade. We thank them for their insights and questions. They have enriched our understanding of the strategies and what it takes for teachers to implement them effectively. We hope this edition reflects all that they have taught us.

Last but not least, we are grateful to our families—parents, spouses, children, dogs, and cats—who supported us in ways that only family can, loving us even when we were stressed and perhaps not in the best humor and understanding when we just had to keep typing.

# Introduction: Instruction That Makes a Difference

"The only way to improve outcomes is to improve instruction."
—Michael Barber & Mona Mourshed, *How the World's Best-Performing School Systems Come Out on Top*

Marisa and her friend Alex, two middle school students, are on the way to their second period classes. Alex complains that Mr. Sommerville's class isn't very interesting, and he doesn't learn much in it.

**Marisa:** I'm looking forward to my class with Ms. Hastings. She makes everyone feel like they can learn math. She always says "hi" to us when we come into class, and she expects us to get right down to work. She has a problem on the board for us to solve on our own, or we check in with our base group.

**Alex:** What's a base group?

**Marisa:** It's a group that stays together for a semester. We do some team building activities and other fun stuff to get to know one another. That makes it easier to speak up in class.

**Alex:** Mr. Sommerville is usually busy at his desk when we come in, and we just talk until a few minutes after the bell. Then he asks us to be quiet, and he starts his lecture. Mostly, we're just bored. Some kids even put their heads down on their desks.

**Marisa:** We'd never do that in Ms. Hastings's class! She'd think we were sick or something. She expects us to do our best every day, and she tells us lots of stories about people who worked

hard and succeeded. She likes us to share stories like that
about ourselves or other people we know. We even keep
track of how much effort we're putting into our work and
how much we're learning. Sometimes I get discouraged, but
Ms. Hastings always says something to help me see what I *do*
know and what I can do to get better.

**Alex:**    I wish Mr. Sommerville was more like Ms. Hastings. Maybe
then I'd care more about learning and get better grades.

Compare Ms. Hastings's and Mr. Sommerville's approaches to teaching.
Ms. Hastings has strong relationships with her students, high expectations for
their performance, and an understanding of the kind of support students need
to succeed in the classroom. Mr. Sommerville seems disconnected from his
students both in terms of personal relationships and in his use of strategies
that will help them learn.

Our goal as authors is to help teachers add to and polish the tools in their
instructional toolkits so they can be more like Ms. Hastings and less like Mr.
Sommerville. To accomplish that goal, we present nine categories of instructional strategies and relevant classroom practices that use them. These nine
categories include

- Setting Objectives and Providing Feedback
- Reinforcing Effort and Providing Recognition
- Cooperative Learning
- Cues, Questions, and Advance Organizers
- Nonlinguistic Representations
- Summarizing and Note Taking
- Assigning Homework and Providing Practice
- Identifying Similarities and Differences
- Generating and Testing Hypotheses

There is evidence that an individual teacher can have a significant effect on
student achievement, even if the school does not (Brophy & Good, 1986; Sanders & Horn, 1994; Wright, Horn, & Sanders, 1997). To ensure that all students
succeed academically, we believe that high-quality instruction must be the
norm and not the exception within schools and across districts. This requires

teachers to develop a common language for instruction and effectively use a common set of instructional strategies that have a high likelihood of increasing student achievement. We offer the strategies in this book as one such set.

We do not claim that these strategies are "silver bullets" or that they will be effective in all circumstances. Rather, they are "best bets" if teachers incorporate them systematically and intentionally as they plan and deliver instruction. Teachers must know what each strategy entails (i.e., its component parts), how and when to use each strategy, and why each works in specific circumstances. To get the most out of this approach, teachers must bring to bear their knowledge of and skill with the instructional strategies, and they must exercise judgment and wisdom with regard to the use of the strategies. As Walberg notes, "The best saw swung as a hammer may do little good" (1999, p. 76).

## Research Behind the Strategies

The strategies featured in this book were identified through a meta-analysis of instruction conducted by McREL (Marzano, 1998) and presented in the first edition of *Classroom Instruction That Works* (Marzano, Pickering, & Pollock, 2001). This second edition builds on that research and incorporates findings from a study that clarifies the concepts related to each of the nine categories identified in the first edition (Beesley & Apthorp, 2010), and it uses an analysis of the literature published since the first edition to provide an updated estimate of each strategy's effect on student achievement. We present these effect sizes as part of the discussion of each strategy.[1]

For the 2010 study, McREL researchers synthesized primary studies for each strategy and calculated a measure of its effects when there were sufficient quantitative data. This approach differs from the original study (Marzano, 1998), which synthesized findings from prior meta-analyses. To update conceptual clarity around each category of strategy, McREL researchers used narrative

---

[1] An effect size expresses the increase or decrease, in standard deviation units, in the outcome (e.g., achievement) for an experimental group (e.g., the group of students who are exposed to a specific instructional technique) versus a control group. Using a statistical conversion table, we can translate effect sizes into percentile point gains. For example, an effect size of 1.00 translates to a 34 point percentile difference that favors students instructed under the experimental conditions. Another interpretation is that, all else being equal, we would expect a student performing at the 50th percentile under the control condition (instruction that does not include the strategy) to improve to the 84th percentile under the experimental condition (instruction that includes the strategy).

reviews, qualitative research, and theoretical literature. For details about the study methodology, see the technical report (Beesley & Apthorp, 2010).[2]

## Organization of the Book

This book, which is organized into four parts, includes information that will help teachers understand what each strategy includes, how to use it, when it is most effective in teaching, and why it works. The first three parts (Chapters 1 through 9) focus on the strategies and include recommended classroom practices, examples of the strategies in use, tips for teaching, and information about using the strategies with today's learners. The tips are drawn from information within each chapter and from our experience working with teachers who are learning about and using these strategies successfully in their own classrooms. The fourth part (Chapter 10) presents specific guidance on how to use the strategies to plan for instruction that targets different types of knowledge. Information on how teachers, principals, and support staff can use this book differently can be found at www.ascd.org/citw.

In the first edition of *Classroom Instruction That Works*, the strategies were presented according to the magnitude of their average effect size (from largest to smallest). That presentation encouraged some schools and districts to focus on the first three or four strategies with the highest effect sizes without regard to *when* those strategies should be used. For example, teachers were asked to focus on identifying similarities and differences as often as possible, yet they found this difficult to do in the early part of a unit when students didn't have a basic understanding of the concepts and vocabulary related to the topic. This focus on the strategies with the highest effect sizes often meant that those at the bottom of the list were disregarded or considered less important. As a result, teachers often minimized their use of key practices that help students activate background knowledge (cues, questions, and advance organizers) and use higher-order thinking skills (generating and testing hypotheses).

In this second edition of *Classroom Instruction That Works*, the strategies are organized and presented within a framework that is geared toward instructional planning. This helps readers learn about each strategy in the context

---

[2] The technical report, *Classroom Instruction That Works, Second Edition, Research Report* is available for free download at www.mcrel.org.

of how it might be used instructionally, and it highlights the point that *all* of the strategies are effective and should be included in instructional planning. This organization also supports our goal of helping teachers use the strategies intentionally. The framework has three components, which were selected because they focus on the key aspects of teaching and learning:

1. Creating the Environment for Learning
2. Helping Students Develop Understanding
3. Helping Students Extend and Apply Knowledge

The strategies in the first component of the framework—Creating the Environment for Learning—are the backdrop for every lesson. When teachers create an environment for learning, they motivate and focus student learning by helping students know what is expected of them, providing students with opportunities for regular feedback on their progress, and assuring students that they are capable of learning challenging content and skills. They also encourage students to actively engage in and "own" their learning, provide opportunities for students to share and discuss their ideas, develop collaboration skills, and learn how to monitor and reflect on their learning.

The second component—Helping Students Develop Understanding—acknowledges that students come to the classroom with prior knowledge and must integrate new learning with what they already know. The strategies included in this component help teachers use students' prior knowledge as scaffolding for new learning. The process of acquiring and integrating information-type knowledge requires students to construct meaning and then organize and store information. Constructing meaning is an active process—students recall prior knowledge, make and verify predictions, correct misconceptions, fill in unstated information, and identify confusing aspects of the knowledge (Marzano & Pickering, 1997). Students organize information by recognizing patterns in the information (e.g., a sequence of events, a description), and they store information most effectively by creating a mental image of it. Acquiring and integrating procedure-type knowledge involves (1) constructing a model of the steps required of the process or skill, (2) developing a conceptual understanding of the process and understanding and practicing its variations, and (3) using the process or skill fluently or without much conscious thought (Marzano & Pickering, 1997).

Strategies in the third component of the framework—Helping Students Extend and Apply Knowledge—emphasize the importance of helping students move beyond "right answer" learning to an expanded understanding and use of concepts and skills in real-world contexts. These strategies help students become more efficient and flexible in using what they have learned. They involve the use of complex reasoning processes, which are necessary for students to use knowledge meaningfully (Marzano & Pickering, 1997). Figure A.1 illustrates where each strategy fits in the framework.

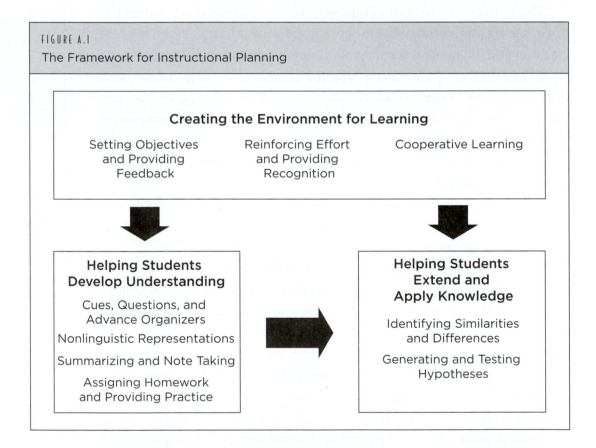

FIGURE A.1
The Framework for Instructional Planning

**Creating the Environment for Learning**

Setting Objectives and Providing Feedback

Reinforcing Effort and Providing Recognition

Cooperative Learning

**Helping Students Develop Understanding**

Cues, Questions, and Advance Organizers

Nonlinguistic Representations

Summarizing and Note Taking

Assigning Homework and Providing Practice

**Helping Students Extend and Apply Knowledge**

Identifying Similarities and Differences

Generating and Testing Hypotheses

## Laying the Foundation

In the remainder of this introduction, we provide some principles of learning that are derived from research and theory on learning and which inform educators' understanding of how students learn. We provide an explanation of current thinking about the skills that are important for students to acquire in the 21st century; the strategies in this book are useful for helping students acquire many of those skills. Finally, we provide information about the importance of teachers' relationships with students in the learning process (which is essential to the first step of the framework).

## Research-based teaching and learning in the 21st century

What does teaching and learning look like as we enter the second decade of the 21st century? Teachers today face classrooms that are increasingly diverse, both culturally and linguistically (Goodwin, Lefkowits, Woempner, & Hubbell, 2011). They must motivate students to attend to learning in environments dominated by external influences such as sports, television, social networking, texting, video games, and the Internet. They must develop new skills or modify existing skills to meet the needs of students who are used to learning through technology.

Linda Darling-Hammond and her colleagues (2008) emphasize that the principles of learning identified by Suzanne Donovan and John Bransford (2005), and paraphrased here, should guide teaching in the 21st century:

1. Students come to the classroom with prior understandings and experiences. To promote student learning, teachers must address and build upon this prior knowledge.
2. Students must have factual and conceptual knowledge in order to develop deep understanding and effectively retrieve and apply knowledge in real-world contexts.
3. Students learn more effectively when they are aware of how they learn and know how to monitor and reflect on their learning.

Focusing on these principles will help teachers prepare students to meet the demands they will face as part of the workforce—solving problems flexibly, thinking critically, and using their knowledge and skills in new situations (Darling-Hammond et al., 2008). The nine categories of instructional strategies (Figure A.2) reflect these principles and help teachers address what is known about learning.

**FIGURE A.2**
The Nine Categories of Instructional Strategies

| Category | Definition |
|---|---|
| **Setting Objectives and Providing Feedback** | Provide students with a direction for learning and with information about how well they are performing relative to a particular learning objective so they can improve their performance. |
| **Reinforcing Effort and Providing Recognition** | Enhance students' understanding of the relationship between effort and achievement by addressing students' attitudes and beliefs about learning. Provide students with abstract tokens of recognition or praise for their accomplishments related to the attainment of a goal. |
| **Cooperative Learning** | Provide students with opportunities to interact with one another in ways that enhance their learning. |
| **Cues, Questions, and Advance Organizers** | Enhance students' ability to retrieve, use, and organize what they already know about a topic. |
| **Nonlinguistic Representations** | Enhance students' ability to represent and elaborate on knowledge using mental images. |
| **Summarizing and Note Taking** | Enhance students' ability to synthesize information and organize it in a way that captures the main ideas and supporting details. |
| **Assigning Homework and Providing Practice** | Extend the learning opportunities for students to practice, review, and apply knowledge. Enhance students' ability to reach the expected level of proficiency for a skill or process. |
| **Identifying Similarities and Differences** | Enhance students' understanding of and ability to use knowledge by engaging them in mental processes that involve identifying ways in which items are alike and different. |
| **Generating and Testing Hypotheses** | Enhance students' understanding of and ability to use knowledge by engaging them in mental processes that involve making and testing hypotheses. |

## Essential skills for 21st century learners

The conversation about 21st century learners has centered on the skills students need to be college and career ready and economically competitive. According to David Conley, one of the key dimensions of college readiness in the 21st century deals with cognitive strategies, which he describes as "patterns of intellectual behavior that lead to the development of mental processes and capabilities necessary for college-level work" (2007, p. 9). These strategies include problem solving, research, analysis, interpretation, reasoning, and precision and accuracy. Conley emphasizes that students develop these skills over time through intentional practice and use, and the skills ultimately lead students to "think about the world in complex ways" (p. 10). Daniel Pink takes another tack when he emphasizes that students cannot rely solely on "left-brain" skills for success in the 21st century. They also need to be able to design innovations, communicate through compelling stories, develop rapport with others, and synthesize seemingly disconnected pieces of information in new ways (Pink, 2005). The Partnership for 21st Century Skills (n.d.) emphasizes that students need specific knowledge in core subjects as well as an understanding of such 21st century themes as global awareness; financial, economic, business, and entrepreneurial literacy; civic literacy; health literacy; and environmental literacy.

Those who advocate for educating the whole child echo much of what is promoted by the Partnership for 21st Century Skills. They support the idea that education today must go beyond the three *R*s of yesterday to encompass a range of skills that will help students function as productive citizens who are health conscious, appreciative of the arts, and aware of the importance of good manners and social skills (Scherer, 2007).

The nine categories of instructional strategies are "best bets" for developing 21st century learners because they help students set personal learning goals, self-check for understanding, access tools and resources for enhancing their understanding, and use what they have learned in real-world contexts. These skills are vital for success in a postindustrial world where it is more important to know how to access information and be a self-motivated learner than it is to memorize content and processes. By using these strategies, teachers can move beyond "teaching content" to teaching students how to learn—that is, find and evaluate content, connect with prior knowledge, and use that knowledge to solve authentic problems. The strategies in this book also help teachers create challenging, emotionally safe learning environments; actively engage students in learning; connect students to teachers and one another in productive ways; and help students develop critical thinking skills that prepare them for higher education and the workforce.

## The importance of student–teacher relationships in the classroom

One of the most important influences on student achievement is the relationship between the teacher and students (Hattie, 2009). If you ask any student what makes a good teacher, the answer is likely to be something that reflects the importance of this relationship. Teachers who have good relationships with students care about students as people and learners. They hold high expectations for their students, convey these expectations to their students, and help their students meet these expectations. They design learning activities that are worthy of students' effort, are relevant to students' lives, and require higher-order thinking (Brophy, 2004). They are warm and empathetic and establish a sense of community within the classroom where they respect students and where students respect them and one another (Goodwin, 2011). When teacher–student relationships are not strong, student learning suffers.

Inherent to establishing a positive learning environment is a growth mind-set, which means teachers view student achievement as something that can be changed through "application and experience" (Dweck, 2006, p. 7). Teachers' words and actions make it clear that student achievement depends on hard work and effort and is not set in stone by past performance. When teachers promote a growth mind-set, they focus students on "self-development, self-motivation, and responsibility" and help them develop the mental determination to continue improving and learning (p. 107). The strategies included in the first section of the organizing framework for this book (Setting Objectives and Providing Feedback, Reinforcing Effort and Providing Recognition, and Cooperative Learning) promote a growth mind-set and help teachers establish positive student–teacher relationships. In addition, these strategies help students develop a belief in their ability to positively affect their learning. This increased self-efficacy motivates students to engage in learning and persist when they encounter difficult content. The strategies in the remaining categories also contribute to positive student–teacher relationships by providing opportunities for higher-order thinking.

# Part I

## Creating the Environment
## for Learning

# 1

# Setting Objectives and Providing Feedback

"The key to making your students' learning experiences worthwhile is to focus your planning on major instructional goals, phrased in terms of desired student outcomes—the knowledge, skills, attitudes, values, and dispositions that you want to develop in your students. Goals, not content coverage or learning processes, provide the rationale for curriculum and instruction."

—Jere Brophy, *Motivating Students to Learn*

Imagine that you have to go to a city you haven't visited before. You know that cities have a variety of services and attractions, but you don't know exactly what you are supposed to do in this particular city. Should you provide a service for someone, gather information about a particular person or place, or do something else? Without a specific objective, you could spend your time on something that isn't important or that makes it difficult to know whether your time in the city was worth the trip.

Being in a classroom without knowing the direction for learning is similar to taking a purposeless trip to an unfamiliar city. Teachers can set objectives to ensure that students' journeys with learning are purposeful. When teachers identify and communicate clear learning objectives, they send the message that there is a focus for the learning activities to come. This reassures students that there is a reason for learning and provides teachers with a focal point for planning instruction. Providing feedback specific to learning objectives helps students improve their performance and solidify their understanding.

Setting objectives and providing feedback work in tandem. Teachers need to identify success criteria for learning objectives so students know when they have achieved those objectives (Hattie & Timperley, 2007). Similarly, feedback should be provided for tasks that are related to the learning objectives; this way, students understand the purpose of the work they are asked to do, build a coherent understanding of a content domain, and develop high levels of skill in a specific domain. In this chapter, we present classroom practices for setting objectives and providing feedback that reassure students that their teacher is focused on helping them succeed.

## Why This Category Is Important

Setting objectives is the process of establishing a direction to guide learning (Pintrich & Schunk, 2002). When teachers communicate objectives for student learning, students can see more easily the connections between what they are doing in class and what they are supposed to learn. They can gauge their starting point in relation to the learning objectives and determine what they need to pay attention to and where they might need help from the teacher or others. This clarity helps decrease anxiety about their ability to succeed. In addition, students build intrinsic motivation when they set personal learning objectives.

Providing feedback is an ongoing process in which teachers communicate information to students that helps them better understand what they are to learn, what high-quality performance looks like, and what changes are necessary to improve their learning (Hattie & Timperley, 2007; Shute, 2008). Feedback provides information that helps learners confirm, refine, or restructure various kinds of knowledge, strategies, and beliefs that are related to the learning objectives (Hattie & Timperley, 2007). When feedback provides explicit guidance that helps students adjust their learning (e.g., "Can you think of another way to approach this task?"), there is a greater impact on achievement, students are more likely to take risks with their learning, and they are more likely to keep trying until they succeed (Brookhart, 2008; Hattie & Timperley, 2007; Shute, 2008).

The results from McREL's 2010 study indicate that the strategies of setting objectives and providing feedback have positive impacts on student achievement. The 2010 study provides separate effect sizes for setting objectives (0.31) and providing feedback (0.76). These translate to percentile gains of 12 points and 28 points, respectively. The first edition of this book reported a combined effect size of 0.61, or a percentile gain of 23 points, for this category. Differences in effect sizes may reflect the different methodologies used in the two studies, as well as the smaller study sample size (four studies related to setting objectives; five studies related to providing feedback) and the specific definitions used in the 2010 study to describe the two strategies.

Studies related to setting objectives emphasize the importance of supporting students as they self-select learning targets, self-monitor their progress, and self-assess their development (Glaser & Brunstein, 2007; Mooney, Ryan, Uhing, Reid, & Epstein, 2005). For example, in the Glaser and Brunstein study (2007), 4th grade students who received instruction in writing strategies and self-regulation strategies (e.g., goal setting, self-assessment, and strategy monitoring) were better able to use their knowledge when planning and revising a story, and they wrote stories that were more complete and of higher quality than the stories of control students and students who received only strategy instruction. In addition, they retained the level of performance they reached at the post-test over time, and when asked to recall parts of an orally presented story, the strategy plus self-regulation students scored higher on the written recall measure than did students in the other two groups.

The studies related to feedback underscore the importance of providing feedback that is instructive, timely, referenced to the actual task, and focused on what is correct and what to do next (Hattie & Timperley, 2007; Shute, 2008). They also address the use of attributional and metacognitive feedback. For example, a study by Kramarski and Zeichner (2001) investigated the use of metacognitive feedback versus results feedback in a 6th grade mathematics class as a way to help students know what to do to improve their performance. Metacognitive feedback was provided by asking questions that served as cues about the content and structure of the problem and ways to solve it. Results feedback provided cues related to the final outcome of the problem. Students who received metacognitive feedback significantly outperformed students who received results feedback, in terms of mathematical achievement and the ability to provide mathematical explanations. They were more likely to provide explanations of their mathematical reasoning, and those explanations were robust—they included both algebraic rules and verbal arguments.

## Classroom Practice for Setting Objectives

At a minimum, setting objectives involves clearly communicating what students are to learn. The classroom practices presented in this chapter emphasize that there are additional actions teachers should take to maximize this strategy's potential for improving student achievement.

There are four recommendations for setting objectives in the classroom:

- Set learning objectives that are specific but not restrictive.
- Communicate the learning objectives to students and parents.
- Connect the learning objectives to previous and future learning.
- Engage students in setting personal learning objectives.

### Set learning objectives that are specific but not restrictive

The process of setting learning objectives begins with knowing the specific standards, benchmarks, and supporting knowledge that students in your school or district are required to learn. State and local standards or curriculum documents are generally the source for this information. Often, standards are written at a fairly general level. If they are not too broad, they might serve as learning objectives at the course or unit level. Often, teachers must "unpack" the statements of knowledge in their standards document to drill down to more specific statements of knowledge and skills that can serve as the focus for instructional design and delivery. For example, as a 3rd grade teacher prepares to design and deliver writing instruction, he or she might encounter the following 3rd grade standard and expectation:

**Standard:** Use the general skills and strategies of the writing process.

**Benchmark:** Write informative/explanatory text to examine a topic and convey ideas and information clearly.

In this example, the standard is written at a very general level. The benchmark statement is more specific and could serve as the learning objective for a unit or portion of a unit. Notice that the benchmark provides detail about what the student must be able to do (write informative/explanatory text) and for what purpose (to examine a topic and convey ideas and information clearly). To identify learning objectives for individual lessons, the teacher might begin by asking the question "What does it mean for students to write informative/ explanatory text to examine a topic and convey ideas and information clearly?" By answering this question, the teacher can determine what students must know, understand, and be able to do.

In this example, the teacher may use the unpacking process to determine that, in order to demonstrate proficiency, students need to be responsible for the entire process of writing a paragraph that groups sentences around a specific topic. This includes

- Generating the topic, instead of receiving the topic from the teacher.
- Understanding the procedure for writing a complete paragraph.
- Demonstrating the ability to write a complete paragraph that includes an introductory sentence, supporting sentences, and a concluding sentence, without the aid of sentence starters or similar assistance.
- Demonstrating the ability to establish and maintain coherence through-out a paragraph by aligning sentences with one another and to the topic.

The teacher uses the knowledge and skills identified through the unpacking process to develop lesson objectives. These objectives explicitly focus instruction on guiding students toward proficiency with the content knowledge and skills expressed in the standards document. Learning objectives should not be so broad that they are meaningless or so narrow that they limit learning or provide few opportunities for differentiation. Figure 1.1 presents examples of learning objectives that are too general, too specific, and appropriately specific.

To provide the guidance that students need, learning objectives should be stated in terms of what students are supposed to learn, not what activity or assignment they are expected to complete. For example, "Understand how white settlers interacted with American Indians" is a learning objective, and "Read pages 14–17 and answer the questions about ways that white settlers interacted with American Indians" is a learning activity. The learning objective is what students should know, understand, or be able to do as a result of completing the learning activity or assignment. Stating learning objectives as statements of knowledge underscores the point that attaining objectives is about acquiring knowledge rather than competing against others (Brophy, 2004).

| FIGURE 1.1 Specificity of Learning Objectives | | |
| --- | --- | --- |
| **Too General** | **Too Specific** | **Appropriately Specific** |
| Understand the fundamental concepts of growth and development. | Describe the function of the respiratory system in three sentences. | Identify basic human body systems and their functions. |
| Use movement concepts and principles in the development of motor skills. | Explain how the principle of overload applies to training for a basketball competition, including at least five details in your explanation. | Apply the physiological principles that govern, maintain, and improve motor skills. |
| Use the process of science inquiry. | Describe three observations about how bean plants grow, using four pictures and at least four numbers. | Record and describe observations with pictures, numbers, or words. |

## Communicate the learning objectives to students and parents

It is important to communicate learning objectives to students explicitly by stating them verbally, displaying them in writing, and calling attention to them throughout a unit or lesson. Clearly stating the learning objectives in student-friendly language helps students focus on what you want them to learn.

Communicating learning objectives to parents helps them understand and become engaged in what their children are learning. When thus informed, parents can then ask their children specific questions, such as "What did you learn today about safety rules in the home and school?" or "What's the most interesting thing about the different states of matter?" Providing multiple options—blogs, text messages, e-mails, letters—for parents to access information about learning objectives sends the message that you value their involvement.

### Example

Administrators at a school in Saipan are experiencing some difficulty as they attempt to identify learning objectives during their regular classroom walkthroughs. They suppose that if *they* are having a difficult time, then students might be experiencing a similar frustration. After teachers understand the administrators' concerns, they decide to denote an area on the classroom boards where the objective can always be found. Each teacher sections off a square of his or her board and then divides the square into two columns. In the left column, teachers write the learning objectives. In the right column, they write the learning activity that the class will focus on during each day or period. Now, anyone who enters the classroom—students, visitors, or administrators—can quickly find the objective and know exactly what is happening each day.

Many teachers now use social media to communicate learning objectives to audiences outside the classroom. For example, a teacher might post weekly objectives on his or her class blog or wiki. Tools such as blogs, websites, and social media pages allow parents to have immediate and accurate access to what is happening in the classroom.

## Connect the learning objectives to previous and future learning

Teachers should explain how learning objectives connect with previous lessons or units or with the larger picture of a particular unit or course (Brophy, 2004; Urdan, 2004). Although most teachers do this naturally, this recommendation is meant to ensure that educators explicitly call students' attention to how the current learning objective is connected to something they have already learned and how they will apply what they are learning now to future studies.

### Example

Mr. Jackson, a 4th grade mathematics teacher, wants to be sure his students understand the connections between what they are doing in a given day's lesson and previous lessons on the same topic. He tells his students, "We've been learning how to add and subtract fractions with like denominators. Today, we're going to apply that knowledge and what we learned about writing equivalent fractions to add fractions with unlike denominators. Eventually, you will be able to apply this knowledge to a cooking activity in which you will combine ingredients to make a Fall Festival cake."

This practice helps Mr. Jackson's students build a more complete mental image of the topic being studied, and it encourages them to commit to the learning objectives.

## Engage students in setting personal learning objectives

Providing opportunities for students to personalize the learning objectives identified by the teacher can increase their motivation for learning (Brophy, 2004; Morgan, 1985; Page-Voth & Graham, 1999). Students feel a greater sense of control over what they learn when they can identify how the learning is relevant to them. In addition, this practice helps students develop self-regulation (Bransford, Brown, & Cocking, 2000). Students who are skilled at self-regulation are able to consciously set goals for their learning and monitor their understanding and progress as they engage in a task. They also can plan appropriately, identify and use necessary resources, respond appropriately to feedback, and evaluate the effectiveness of their actions. Acquiring these skills helps students become independent lifelong learners.

Many students do not have experience with writing their own learning objectives, so it is important for teachers to model the process and provide students with feedback when they are first learning how to set their own learning objectives (White, Hohn, & Tollefson, 1997). Teachers can guide students in the process by

- Providing them with sentence stems such as "I know that . . . but I want to know more about . . ." and "I want to know if . . ." Younger students can write "I can" or "I will" statements.
- Asking them to complete a K-W-L chart as a way to record what they know (K) about the topic, what they want (W) to know as a result of the unit or lesson, and what they learned (L) as a result of the unit or lesson (Ogle, 1986). Students can complete the *L* section throughout the unit

or lesson. Adding a column labeled "What I Think I Know" reduces stress about being correct and expands students' thinking.

- Checking their learning objectives to ensure they are meaningful and attainable within the given time period and with available resources.

If students do not have enough prior knowledge to set personal learning objectives at the beginning of a unit, delay this task until they have engaged in some of the unit's learning activities. If students struggle with setting personal learning objectives, ask them to talk to a few other students to gather some ideas, or provide some examples and invite them to select one of them.

Studies have shown that "contracts" can have positive effects on students' ability to set objectives for their learning (Brophy, 2004; Greenwood, 2002; Kahle & Kelly, 1994; Miller & Kelley, 1994; Tomlinson, 2001). These contracts provide students with control over their learning and provide opportunities for teachers to differentiate instruction to better accommodate students' learning needs (Tomlinson, 1995). As illustrated in Figure 1.2, contracts can include teacher-identified or student-identified learning objectives. They can take the form of a learning plan that provides options for the kinds of activities students do on particular days and at specific times. In addition, they also provide students with guidance about what they need to accomplish, help students organize their time, and provide ongoing opportunities for students to seek or provide their own feedback.

In this example, elementary students are learning about Earth's cycles. Specifically, they are working on the learning objective "Knows how features on the Earth's surface are constantly changed by a combination of slow and rapid processes (e.g., slow processes, such as weathering, erosion, transport, and deposition of sediment caused by waves, wind, water, and ice; rapid processes, such as landslides, volcanic eruptions, and earthquakes." As shown by Figure 1.2, this student wants to know why some changes on Earth happen steadily, whereas others happen irregularly. He plans to research this information by watching a few online streaming videos recommended by his teacher and by conducting targeted Internet searches.

| FIGURE 1.2 | | | | | | | |
|---|---|---|---|---|---|---|---|
| **Sample Learning Contract for Elementary Science** | | | | | | | |
| **Learning Objectives** | **Class** | **Personal** | **Activities I Will Do to Achieve the Objective** | | | | |
| | | | Read Materials | Learning Center | Watch Video | Discuss with a Partner | Other *(specify)* |
| Explain changes in the real world using a model. | X | | | X | | X | |
| Know that changes are steady or irregular. | X | | X | | X | | |
| Know that some changes are repetitive. | X | | X | X | X | | |
| I want to know why some changes are steady and some are irregular. | | X | | | | X | *Find information on the Internet.* |

## Classroom Practice for Providing Feedback

By providing students with feedback that is corrective, timely, and focused on criteria, and by involving them in the feedback process, teachers can create a classroom environment that fosters and supports learning. The classroom practices featured in this chapter emphasize that the goal of providing feedback is to give students information about their performance relative to a particular learning objective so they can improve their performance and understand themselves better as learners.

There are four recommendations for classroom practice with regard to providing feedback:

- Provide feedback that addresses what is correct and elaborates on what students need to do next.
- Provide feedback appropriately in time to meet students' needs.
- Provide feedback that is criterion referenced.
- Engage students in the feedback process.

### Provide feedback that addresses what is correct and elaborates on what students need to do next

This practice underscores the link between learning objectives and feedback. Providing specific feedback that helps students know how to improve their performance requires teachers to identify and understand the learning objectives (Stiggins, 2001). If teachers do not understand the learning objectives, it is difficult for them to provide students with information about what good performance or high-quality work looks like.

Feedback should help students understand what was correct as well as contain specifics about what was incorrect. If a student's performance falls short because he or she is operating from faulty interpretations or hypotheses, feedback should make this clear (Hattie & Timperley, 2007). For example, if students assume that seasons are due to Earth's distance from the sun, the teacher's feedback should include information that helps students understand that seasons are a consequence of Earth's tilt. Providing this kind of information helps students fill in missing information and clarify misunderstandings.

Effective feedback should also provide information about how close students come to meeting the criterion and details about what they need to do to attain the next level of performance (Shirbagi, 2007; Shute, 2008). Teachers can provide elaboration in the form of worked examples, questions, or prompts—such as "What's this problem all about?"—or as information about the correct answer (Kramarski & Zeichner, 2001; Shute, 2008).

#### Example

Mrs. Wang is working individually with Sophia, a student struggling with writing a persuasive essay. Sophia is passionate about her views of reducing waste and recycling, yet her current essay comes across as "ranting" without much information to back up her views. As they work through the essay, Mrs. Wang's feedback commends Sophia's enthusiasm for her topic and helps her rewrite the essay as a call to action rather than as a diatribe. At the end of the session, Mrs. Wang says to Sophia, "I think our next step is to show readers what first intrigued you to take action. You mention that you saw a video about the amount of waste going to landfills. Perhaps we could find some exact numbers about how much trash we produce. That would help readers understand your passion for creating change."

In this way, Mrs. Wang gives specific and helpful feedback to Sophia, and she also guides her student to future steps that are needed.

## Provide feedback in time to meet students' needs

As in many other areas of life, timing is everything (or at least important) when giving feedback. Recent research indicates that the timing of feedback depends to some extent on the nature of the task and on whether students are high performing or low performing (Shute, 2008). When students are engrossed in figuring out a difficult task, feedback should be delayed; however, when students can use feedback to complete a task, immediacy helps. Providing immediate feedback can encourage students to practice, and it helps them make connections between what they do and the results they achieve. Delaying feedback may encourage development of cognitive and metacognitive processing for high-performing students, yet it may cause frustration for struggling and less-motivated students (Clariana & Koul, 2006; Shute, 2008). Further, some studies indicate that students may benefit from delayed feedback when they are learning concepts and from immediate feedback when they are acquiring procedural skills (Franzke, Kintsch, Caccamise, Johnson, & Dooley, 2005; Mathan & Koedinger, 2002; Shute, 2008).

### Example

Zach, a 3rd grader, is working on his multiplication facts. His teacher provides multiple activities that are fun and motivating and that give Zach timely feedback on his progress. Several times during the week, Zach is given 15 minutes to perform multiplication problems via computer games, board games, or flash cards. Each session gives him immediate feedback on whether his answers are correct (and if he is not, the correct answer is provided). At the end of the week, Zach takes a timed quiz. His teacher grades the quiz during lunch and then returns it to Zach so he can record the time and score on a chart he has been keeping. This timely feedback and tracking experience help Zach see how he is progressing in his attempt to master this particular skill.

## Provide feedback that is criterion referenced

Feedback should address the knowledge that students are supposed to learn and provide information that helps them know what needs to be done to improve their performance. Obviously, feedback shouldn't be personal ("You're smart"), but, rather, it should address performance on a task and provide specific guidance for improvement ("Your response lacks details and includes some inaccurate information. Check the facts about this event, and add details to describe the reasons the event occurred.").

One approach to providing criterion-referenced feedback is to use a rubric. A rubric is a scoring guide that describes levels of performance for a particular skill or concept. The number of levels included in a rubric can vary, but there should be at least one level beyond the level designated as "acceptable" or "proficient" performance. Rubrics that relate to information-type knowledge (vocabulary terms, facts, details, generalizations, principles, concepts) focus on the extent of understanding of the information. They might include criteria related to the level of detail students know or the completeness and accuracy of understanding.

Rubrics for skill- or process-type knowledge (adding fractions, reading, writing) focus on whether students can perform the skill or process without error and with fluency. Teachers should provide examples of work at each level of performance to help students better understand what high-quality work looks like. Figure 1.3 provides examples of general rubrics for information and skills/processes. Teachers can adapt these rubrics for specific content, skills, and processes. For more information about developing rubrics, see *Classroom Assessment for Student Learning: Doing it Right—Using it Well* (Stiggins, Arter, Chappuis, & Chappuis, 2006).

### Example

Mrs. McWherter, a 6th grade language arts teacher, is working with her students on writing biographies. She and Mr. Thompson, the social

### FIGURE 1.3
### General Rubric Examples

**Rubric for Information-Type Knowledge**

| Performance Level | Performance Description |
|---|---|
| 4 | The student has a complete and detailed understanding of the information important to the topic. |
| 3 | The student has a complete understanding of the information important to the topic but not in great detail. |
| 2 | The student has an incomplete understanding of the topic and/or misconceptions about some of the information. |
| 1 | The student understands very little about the topic or has misconceptions about most of the information. |
| 0 | No judgment can be made about the student's understanding of the topic. |

**Rubric for Processes and Skills-Type Knowledge**

| Performance Level | Performance Description |
|---|---|
| 4 | The student can perform the skill or process important to the topic with no significant errors and with fluency. In addition, the student understands the key features of the process. |
| 3 | The student can perform the skill or process important to the topic without making significant errors. |
| 2 | The student makes some significant errors when performing the skill or process important to the topic but still accomplishes a rough approximation of the skill or process. |
| 1 | The student makes so many errors in performing the skill or process important to the topic that he or she cannot actually perform the skill or process. |
| 0 | No judgment can be made about the student's ability to perform the skill or process. |

studies teacher, combine efforts as their students learn about heroes of the American Revolution. Students are supposed to not only research a hero or heroine of their choice but also use what they learn to write a biography of that person. In Mrs. McWherter's class, students go through the criteria of what constitutes an informative and engaging biography. In Mr. Thompson's class, students go through the process of gathering information about an appropriate hero. In this way, students use rubrics pertaining to both procedural and declarative knowledge, which helps them address all components of the project.

## Engage students in the feedback process

Students can provide some of their own feedback and provide feedback to peers. Providing students with opportunities to reflect on their own performance and exchange feedback with peers can help them become lifelong learners (Glaser & Brunstein, 2007; Mooney et al., 2005). It is important to remember, however, that the purpose of peer feedback is for students to clarify for one another what was correct or incorrect about their responses. Students should not give one another grades or scores. Rather, they should serve as "reviewers" who help determine what might be lacking in their performance.

Teachers can involve students in the feedback process by asking them to keep track of their performance as learning occurs during a unit or course. For example, students might graph their progress or write weekly journal entries (or learning blogs) that describe what they've learned and how well they've learned it. If students have not had much experience engaging in the feedback process, they will be more successful if you provide them with templates or protocols that structure their feedback and model the process, as in the example that follows.

### Example

Mr. Carson is working with his 2nd grade students as they learn to write biographies. He wishes to begin incorporating a self- and peer-feedback component to his students' writing cycle. He begins by having a discussion about what type of feedback is helpful and feels rewarding versus the type of feedback that isn't very helpful or even feels discouraging. The class agrees that feedback such as "that's great" makes them feel good, but it really doesn't help them know what is correct and what needs to be corrected. They also agree that words need to be chosen carefully when giving feedback so that feelings aren't hurt.

Mr. Carson then reviews with the class what they have learned about biographies. As he talks, he holds up several biographies that they've read together, and he reminds students of some of the details they read. Finally, he is ready to give his assignment: Each student should research a person that he or she admires and then write a short biographical paragraph about this person. Mr. Carson then hands out a rubric to each student and goes over the criteria for the paragraph. Finally, he provides students with a template that helps them reflect on their own learning and give and receive peer feedback (see Downloadable Figure 1). By using this tool, Mr. Carson scaffolds the peer-feedback process for students and lays the groundwork for future collaborative projects.

## Setting Objectives and Providing Feedback with Today's Learners

Providing opportunities for students to personalize their learning objectives helps them find relevant, real-world applications of what they are learning. By engaging students in setting personal learning objectives, teachers enable them to take control of their own learning, which increases their intrinsic motivation. The International Society for Technology in Education's (ISTE) National Educational Technology Standards (NETS) for students echo this motivational aspect of control in their standards for creativity and innovation (2007).

Providing students with opportunities for self- and peer assessment speaks to these 21st century skills. By allocating time for students to reflect upon their own learning and to give and receive feedback from peers, we help them develop skills they will need throughout their K–12 years, in college, and in the workplace. The tools available now (e.g., survey tools, blogs, wikis) strongly amplify students' and teachers' abilities to access, collaborate, and get feedback on their work. Encouraging students to use the many resources available online and through social media and engage in the feedback process helps them become self-directed learners. Students could post their writing to a blog and solicit feedback, or they could create a rubric and ask peers to give feedback on their writing with an online form. Teachers could provide young students with a simple graphic organizer (see Figure 1.4) in which they assess their own work, ask for peer feedback, and receive feedback from the teacher.

Blogs and tools such as VoiceThread, which provide platforms for asynchronous, two-way communication, are excellent ways for students to provide feedback. During their early experiences with peer feedback, students often receive the most benefit if they use protocols that structure their feedback so it is meaningful and constructive. For examples of protocols that can be used in their current forms or modified for student use, see the Reciprocal Revision lesson plan from www.ReadWriteThink.org or any of the resources available on the National School Reform Faculty website (www.nsrfharmony.org). When this type of open feedback and sharing becomes the norm, students learn key habits that will help them become self-directed teachers and learners.

| FIGURE 1.4 Graphic Organizer for Self- and Peer Feedback | | | |
| --- | --- | --- | --- |
| **Learning Objective** | **My Feedback** | **My Partner's Feedback** | **My Teacher's Feedback** |
| I will understand how the interactions of air masses create fronts as they move across oceans and land and how those fronts serve as areas for the development of thunderstorms, tornadoes, and hurricanes. | When I looked at the rubric, I decided that I earned a 2 because I can explain how thunderstorms and tornadoes form, but I don't really understand what causes a tropical storm to become a hurricane. | Your explanations all seemed accurate, except for the one on hurricanes. You seemed a little confused about how they got started and got bigger. | You earned a 2.5 on the rubric. You provided an accurate explanation of how thunderstorms and tornadoes form, but your explanation about the difference between tropical storms and hurricanes was inaccurate and included only a few specific details. |

## Tips for Teaching Using Setting Objectives and Providing Feedback

1. State learning objectives in simple language and in terms of knowledge rather than learning activities.
2. Relate the learning objectives to things that are personally relevant to students.
3. Model for students how to set their own learning objectives, and provide feedback on the learning objectives they set.

4. Periodically check student understanding of the learning objectives (e.g., ask them to write in their journals or on notecards about their understanding of the learning objectives).

5. Select content sources, discussion questions, activities, assignments, and assessment methods according to how well they help students achieve learning objectives.

6. Provide students with information about what good performance or high-quality work looks like well before an assessment.

7. Provide students with feedback as soon after the event as possible and throughout a unit of instruction—not just at the end of a unit.

8. After providing students with feedback about what they did correctly and what they need to do to improve performance, provide opportunities for them to continue working on the task until they succeed.

9. Consider using technology to increase the rate of feedback, help organize it, and document it for further reflection.

# 2

# Reinforcing Effort and Providing Recognition

"The key to rewarding effectively is to do so in ways that support students' motivation to learn and do not encourage them to conclude that they engage in academic activities only to earn rewards."

—Jere Brophy, *Motivating Students to Learn*

How many times have you felt frustrated because students didn't seem to be motivated? Most teachers would agree that student motivation is a key ingredient in learning. Research supports this belief—studies indicate a link between motivation and achievement (Eccles, Wigfield, & Schiefele, 1998; Greene, Miller, Crowson, Duke, & Akey, 2004; Phan, 2009). What is this link? Motivation influences how much effort students expend and how long they persist in working on tasks, and the amount of effort and persistence that students put forth influences their level of academic success (Bouffard, Boisvert, Vezeau, & Larouche, 1995; Elliot, McGregor, & Gable, 1999).

Motivation influences achievement, but what influences motivation? Student motivation is complex; many variables influence whether students engage and persist in tasks, including teacher, parent, and cultural beliefs (Wigfield & Eccles, 2000). Students' beliefs about their own competence and whether they have any control over the outcome of a task, as well as their interest in the task and the reason *why* they are interested, also influence student engagement and persistence (Bandura, 1986; Covington, 1992; Pintrich & Schrauben, 1992; Pintrich & Schunk, 2002). In this chapter, we focus on two strategies that are related to motivation: reinforcing effort and providing recognition. These two strategies affect one or more of the following student variables:

- Self-efficacy: beliefs about one's competency.
- Control beliefs: beliefs about one's ability to influence what is happening or will happen.
- Intrinsic motivation: motivation that comes from an individual's desire for self-satisfaction or pleasure in completing the task rather than from an external source, such as a reward.
- Task value: beliefs about reasons for doing a task.

## Why This Category Is Important

When teachers reinforce effort, they translate the belief that all students can learn into actions that help make that belief a reality. Reinforcing effort is a process that involves explicitly teaching students about the relationship between effort and achievement and acknowledging students' efforts when they work hard to achieve. When teachers emphasize this connection, they help students develop a sense of control over their academic learning. Recognizing students' efforts along the way to achieving a goal helps them strengthen their resolve to complete the task or internalize the learning. As students see the results of working hard, they change their attitudes and beliefs about themselves and about their ability to learn. They often become more tenacious and resilient; they will persevere when a task is difficult and success doesn't come immediately. Students' increased sense of competence and control contributes to a positive learning environment and their motivation to learn.

Providing recognition is the process of acknowledging students' attainment of specific goals. Some teachers wonder if providing recognition, particularly in the form of praise, is the right thing to do. They are right to wonder; some research on praise and recognition has shown negative effects on intrinsic motivation (Henderlong & Lepper, 2002; Kamins & Dweck, 1999). Other research indicates that when teachers use an approach that bases student success on mastery of the task (i.e., a mastery-oriented approach) rather than on comparison to others' performance, praise can be used to promote student engagement and decrease behavioral problems (Moore-Partin, Robertson,

Maggin, Oliver, & Wehby, 2010; Simonson, Fairbanks, Briesch, Myers, & Sugai, 2008). Furthermore, praise can influence intrinsic motivation if students perceive the praise to be sincere and if the praise promotes self-determination, encourages students to attribute their performance to causes they can control, and establishes attainable goals and standards (Henderlong & Lepper, 2002). Praise that is more person- or ability-oriented (rather than task- or process-oriented) can have unintended negative effects on intrinsic motivation. When students have setbacks in the domain that was praised, they may think they have lost their ability and react with helplessness. Therefore, teachers must use praise with caution.

Recognition and praise may have a more direct impact on socioemotional indicators—such as self-efficacy (beliefs about one's competency), effort, persistence, and motivation—than on learning. As a result, teachers may not see immediate academic improvements from the effective use of recognition and praise; however, the link between positive socioemotional indicators and learning suggests that fostering the former will have positive effects on the latter over time (Bouffard et al., 1995; Elliot et al., 1999; Greene et al., 2004; Phan, 2009).

McREL researchers found few primary studies related to reinforcing effort and providing recognition that met the criteria for inclusion in the 2010 study. The studies that were included indicated small to negligible effects for the strategies. The researchers were not able to compute separate effect sizes for reinforcing effort and providing recognition, because the identified studies did not include enough data. The earlier study that contributed to the first edition of this text reported a composite effect size of 0.80 when combining studies on the two strategies. For the 2010 study, however, the researchers found that the two strategies were broadly defined in the literature, and they concluded that it would be inappropriate to analyze them together. Therefore, they did not compute an effect size for the combined strategies.

McREL researchers found no other meta-analyses related to reinforcing effort and providing recognition published since the first edition of *Classroom Instruction That Works*. As a result, the classroom practices discussed in this chapter reflect the descriptive analyses of current studies and the practices described in the first edition of this book. For example, one study underscores what can happen when praise is used inappropriately (Horner & Gaither, 2004). This study looked at the effect of a teacher modeling effort in 2nd grade mathematics classrooms. In addition to modeling problem solving with effort and using self-talk as a self-monitoring strategy, the teacher in the experimental group provided feedback on effort. Students in the experimental group decreased attribution of outcomes to factors outside their control (e.g., luck), but they did not increase attributions to effort or perform better on a mathematics assessment than students in the control group did.

The authors suggest that one possible explanation for these results is that the teacher provided feedback that pointed out inaccurate answers and followed up with personal noninstructive feedback (e.g., "If you try harder, you will be able to get the right answer."). Such feedback is ineffective because it focuses on what is incorrect rather than what is correct, and it does not provide information that will help students increase their effort, engagement, or belief in their ability to use the appropriate strategies to understand and accomplish the task (Hattie & Timperley, 2007).

## Classroom Practice for Reinforcing Effort

To use the reinforcing effort strategy effectively, teachers must understand the relationship between effort and achievement and the importance of consistently exposing students to information related to effort. They also must know that students can be taught the importance of effort and what it means to expend effort productively. This section includes three practices for reinforcing effort that reflect these points:

- Teach students about the relationship between effort and achievement.
- Provide students with explicit guidance about exactly what it means to expend effort.
- Ask students to keep track of their effort and achievement.

### Teach students about the relationship between effort and achievement

Teaching about effort can positively influence students' thinking, behavior, and beliefs about their ability to succeed if it helps students understand that success comes because of effort and that they control the amount of effort they put forth. Successful students know that other people, luck, and ability are not "dependable" keys to success—effort is. In other words, they know that other people can help them succeed, but other people can also stand in the way of their success. They understand that it never hurts to be lucky, but luck is not something anyone can count on. They know that ability can make school, sports, or work easier, but few people have high ability in all areas. They know that many successful people are successful because they put forth effort, not because they have high ability, luck, or other people's help. Knowing the relationship between effort and achievement empowers students to be active participants in their own learning.

Students are not likely to change their beliefs overnight about what leads to success. As a result, teachers should regularly incorporate the relationship between effort and achievement in their lessons. Stories, whether about oneself or others (as in the examples that follow), are a powerful mechanism for enhancing student understanding about effort and achievement.

### Example #1

Members of the USA Swimming team at the 2008 Summer Olympics found themselves at the center of a controversy related to their swimsuits. The media was filled with stories that attributed the team's success to the innovative suits. After one relay, a reporter asked a swimmer how the suits were increasing speeds. The swimmer politely explained that he and his teammates practiced at all hours of the day. He shared an account of one teammate's "experiment" with the new suit. He threw one of the suits into the pool only to find that it didn't move. Smiling, he said, "It's not the suit, it's the swimmer who has dedicated hours to practicing that makes the suit move and win."

### Example #2

E'Stephen Garcia was not quite 16 when he watched a friend shoot and kill a convenience store worker. Moving between the homes of his divorced parents, in and out of trouble, behind in his high school credits, and on the verge of going to jail, E'Stephen realized that it was up to him to make something of his life. Through hard work, he graduated from high school on schedule, joined the Army, and eventually went to West Point and studied medicine. When he served as the student-selected speaker at his commencement exercise from West Point, his fellow cadets could not believe that the person they knew was the young man in the story. Today, E'Stephen is a respected doctor, husband, and father. Through consistent effort, E'Stephen completely turned his life around.

Numerous stories about people overcoming odds and becoming successful through their determination and effort are found in newspapers and magazines, on TV broadcasts, on the Internet, and in students' own experiences. Teachers can provide students with ongoing engagement by sharing examples of effort, asking students to share examples, and designing lessons that include a discussion of effort.

## Provide students with explicit guidance about what it means to expend effort

Have you ever heard a student who failed a test say, "I should at least get some credit for all the effort I put into this." We've just said that there is a positive relationship between effort and achievement, so how can it be that some students put forth a great deal of effort and the results are so poor? One explanation is that their understanding of what it means to put forth effort is incomplete or inappropriate for particular situations. Teachers can help students develop an operational definition for what it means to work hard by being explicit about the actions and behaviors associated with effort in a variety of academic situations. For example, a teacher might tell students that working hard while taking notes involves paying attention to what is being said and linking what they hear to what they already know. It also involves summarizing information and making sense of it, rather than trying to write down every word without thinking about what those words mean. Similarly, a teacher who wants students to work well in groups will explicitly teach or succinctly remind students what it looks like, sounds like, and feels like to do so. In this case, students make sure their group members understand the task, complete the work assigned, stay on topic, manage their time well, and ask questions when they are stuck. Explicit information about what it means to expend effort in particular situations, as in the following example, directs students' attention to the actions and behaviors they need to display to be successful.

### Example

Ms. Shah's sophomore geography class is reviewing the questions that appeared on a recent test about Africa. Ashton raises his hand and says, "The problem for me is that I studied for the test, but you didn't ask the right questions." The class laughs at this comment, but Ms. Shah sees a teachable moment. She asks Ashton how he had studied. He replies that he skimmed through the text a few times on the bus and also had talked to Jessica to see what she knew about African countries. A few of the other students in class nod their heads in agreement. Ms. Shah replies, "I'm curious about how many of you used the effort rubric that I provided a few weeks ago to guide your preparation for the test." A few students say they had looked at it; most look a little sheepish.

Ms. Shah realizes it might have been a good idea for her to remind students about the rubric before the test, but all is not lost. She asks students to use the rubric (Figure 2.1) to rate their test preparation effort and compare that rating to their test grades; She opens an online survey on her laptop and asks students to anonymously enter their test scores in the first column and their test prep effort scores in the second column. After the class completes this task, Ms. Shah creates a line graph of the data, and her students are able to see that those who rated their test prep effort as a 1 or 2 generally scored lower than those who rated their prep effort as a 3 or 4.

## Ask students to keep track of their effort and achievement

Once students are clear about what it means to expend effort, teachers can ask them to track their effort in relation to their achievement. Such monitoring helps students focus on the learning objective, on what it takes to achieve that objective, and on their progress toward doing so. Asking students to discuss

| FIGURE 2.1 | | | |
| :--- | :--- | :--- | :--- |
| **Effort Rubric for Test Preparation** | | | |
| **4: Excellent** | **3: Good** | **2: Emerging** | **1: Unsatisfactory** |
| I reread the text and compared the text to my notes, adding to my notes as needed. I sought help from others when I didn't understand and met with a study partner to review and discuss my understanding of key ideas. | I reviewed the text and my notes and added to my notes as needed. I sought help if I didn't understand something. | I skimmed through the text and looked at my notes. | I read my notes once. |

what they are learning about the relationship between their own efforts and achievement provides opportunities to reinforce the control that students have over their own learning.

## Example

Mr. Sebastian's 3rd graders are learning how to write explanatory texts to examine a topic and convey ideas and information. To succeed at writing such texts, students have to be able to introduce a topic and develop it with facts, definitions, and details; use linking words and phrases to connect ideas; and write a conclusion. Mr. Sebastian provides his students with the rubric he will use to score their writing and asks them to talk about what it might mean to put forth effort to produce high-quality explanatory texts. Based on the discussion, the students develop a checklist they can then use to rate their effort on each assignment. Students earn a rating of 0 to 4, depending on the number of items from the checklist they address. They also complete a chart that includes their effort and achievement scores for each assignment (see Figure 2.2).

At the end of the unit on writing explanatory texts, Mr. Sebastian provides his students with the following prompts and asks them to write in their journals about what they will do differently during the next unit, based on what they learned about the relationship between effort and achievement in the current unit.

- I used the effort checklist to . . .
- I learned that I am willing to put forth effort when . . .
- Something that helps me put forth the effort I need to do well is . . .

When Mr. Sebastian reviews his students' journals, he gains insight into how they think about the relationship between effort and achievement, and he is able to identify students who might need additional help to recognize that connection.

FIGURE 2.2
Tracking the Relationship Between Effort and Achievement

| Assignment | Effort | Achievement |
| --- | --- | --- |
| Introducing a Topic | 3 | 3 |
| Developing a Topic with Facts, Definitions, and Details | 2 | 1 |
| Using Linking Words and Phrases | 4 | 3 |
| Writing a Conclusion | 3 | 4 |
| Writing an Explanatory Text | 3 | 3 |

## Classroom Practice for Providing Recognition

Most people like to be recognized for their efforts, whether the recognition comes in the form of praise or as something concrete. Nevertheless, providing recognition must be done appropriately, or it can have negative consequences (Alderman, 2008; Brophy, 2004). The recommendations for practice provided in this section describe ways to ensure that recognition has a positive effect on student motivation and achievement.

There are three recommended practices for providing recognition:

- Promote a mastery-goal orientation.
- Provide praise that is specific and aligned with expected performance and behaviors.
- Use concrete symbols of recognition.

## Promote a mastery-goal orientation

When teachers adopt a mastery-goal orientation, they emphasize learning and meeting goals rather than comparing students' performances (i.e., performance orientation). This doesn't mean that performance is unimportant; rather, it acknowledges that overemphasizing performance can lead to a decrease in self-efficacy, persistence, help-seeking, and effort along with an increase in learned helplessness (Alderman, 2008). A mastery-oriented environment can lead to increased achievement because it helps teachers increase students' self-efficacy, intrinsic motivation, and task value (Greene et al., 2004; Walker, Greene, & Mansell, 2006). Intrinsic motivation, defined as motivation from the task itself, is associated with challenge seeking, confidence, and persistence, which encourage the kind of engagement associated with deep learning (Deci & Ryan, 1985; Ryan & Deci, 2000).

A mastery-goal orientation makes the learning environment more predictable—students know what they need to do to succeed. Teachers can define what it means to expend effort to achieve the goal, and students can expend that effort. If students don't succeed, they can examine their effort and achievement to determine what else they need to do to improve their performance. Students know they will be recognized for their achievement related to the goal rather than for their performance relative to other students. The former provides a sense of control; the latter does not.

A mastery-goal orientation allows teachers to design tasks that are appropriate for students at different levels of learning and to personalize recognition when students accomplish their tasks. This is particularly important for struggling students who might perceive that they have few chances for success or recognition because they have a history of academic failure. These students believe they can't be successful and may be reluctant to engage and persist in tasks that they perceive as difficult (Diperna, 2006; Schunk, 1999; Walker, 2003; Zimmerman, 2000). Teachers can provide these students with some initial tasks that are challenging but not beyond their capabilities. After students are successful with these tasks, teachers then provide them with recognition and gradually present more challenging tasks and link new work to these past successes (Margolis & McCabe, 2004).

### Example

Ms. Roberts wants her high school social studies students to focus on learning, not on proving they have more ability than other students. To emphasize the learning orientation in her classroom, Ms. Roberts explains the intended outcomes of each lesson and learning activity, and she provides opportunities for her students to set their own learning objectives related to the unit and lesson topics. She knows that students are more likely to focus on learning if they are provided with tasks that are intrinsically engaging and connect to their backgrounds and interests. To learn about her students' interests, Ms. Roberts talks informally with each student, and she asks them to complete a questionnaire. Knowing that high school students also have social goals, sometimes she provides opportunities for her students to form cooperative learning groups that are based on friendship or interests. To encourage all students to work hard and achieve, she recognizes everyone for his or her efforts and accomplishments. She treats mistakes as expected parts of the learning process, she helps students attribute success to their use of effective strategies, and she links failure to ineffective strategies. When students are stuck, she provides hints or asks questions that help them think about the task from a different perspective and continue working on it. All of these actions help Ms. Roberts establish a learning community in which students know that learning, not showing that they are better than other students, is what is important.

## Provide praise that is specific and aligned with expected performance and behaviors

How you praise, what you praise, and when you praise matters. Praise must be sincere. If students perceive that praise is not sincere, they will discount it, and there will be no opportunity for it to have a positive effect on motivation (Henderlong & Lepper, 2002). Students might view praise that is overly effusive or very general (e.g., "You always do such wonderful work.") as insincere (Brophy, 2004). The same is true if a teacher's words of praise do not match his or her nonverbal behavior or if it appears that the praise is given to control or manipulate student behavior (Brophy, 2004; Henderlong & Lepper, 2002). Use praise intentionally but sparingly—praise for every small accomplishment can be viewed as praise that is insincere.

Praise should support students' motivation to learn by helping them attribute their efforts to their motivation and their accomplishments to their efforts (Brophy, 2004). To do that, praise should be specific and focus on students' attainment of established goals for performance or behavior. Praise should provide informative feedback about the effort and care that students put into their work, the progress that students make in understanding content or performing skills, or outstanding aspects of their accomplishments (Brophy, 2004). When teachers praise students for tasks that are very easy to accomplish, they send a message of low expectations that can undermine achievement.

Students might reject praise if it is delivered in the presence of peers or if it is overused (Hattie & Timperley, 2007). Students, particularly those in middle and high school, prefer to receive praise outside the range of others' hearing. They will ignore praise if it seems to be random, unsystematic, or disconnected from their efforts or accomplishments (Brophy, 2004). Further, praise may have negative consequences if it is provided in ways that are inconsistent with students' cultural norms. The examples that follow illustrate an effective use of praise.

### Example #1

Samantha worried about being successful in middle school. She had not developed good study habits in elementary school, and she wasn't sure where to begin now that she was an older student. As Samantha entered her 6th grade classes, she noticed that every teacher provided information about effort and recognized students for their hard work and accomplishments. For example, in science class, Samantha's teacher stopped at her table and said, "Congratulations, Samantha. You struggled with using a microscope properly, but you asked questions when you didn't understand, and now your efforts are paying off. Keep working hard; you will find more and more success."

### Example #2

During Rojelio's social studies class, his teacher stopped by his desk and spoke to him quietly, saying, "I know comparing the cultures of the three European countries was difficult, but you persevered until you completed the comparison matrix. You worked well with your partner to stay on task and manage your time. Your efforts are paying off and will help you when you work on the unit project next week."

## Use concrete symbols of recognition

Like praise, tangible rewards can have a positive effect on intrinsic motivation if they are tied to accomplishment of objectives (Henderlong & Lepper, 2002). Using rewards to recognize the quality of students' work and their progress toward the learning goal, rather than task participation or completion, can promote self-efficacy and improved performance (Alderman, 2008). Further, tying rewards to accomplishments helps students understand that they are not completing a task merely for the reward. Teachers can use various concrete, symbolic tokens of recognition such as stickers, coupons, awards, treats, or other types of prizes. Rewards of this type can be helpful to develop initial interest in a skill whose value might not be apparent until students have used it for a while or until the student masters it. Such rewards are better used with routine tasks or ones that require rote learning (e.g., multiplication facts) rather than with those that require creativity or discovery (Brophy, 2004).

## Example

Ms. Raintree knows that her middle school band students have many things on their minds, and practicing their instruments after school probably doesn't rank high among them. She asks students to record themselves playing a short piece of music and then talks to students about the importance of practicing. She helps them think about strategies to organize their time after school so they can practice on a regular basis, and she encourages them to set a goal to practice every day. Students keep track of the amount of time they practice and what they practice (e.g., scales or a specific piece of music) each day in a journal. Every Monday for six weeks, students report to Ms. Raintree about how much they practice. Students who meet their goal for the week, as well as those who come closer to meeting their goal than they did during the previous week, receive a prize: musical-themed stickers or small party favors in the form of toy instruments. At the end of six weeks, Ms. Raintree asks students to record themselves playing another piece of music and to compare their performance (using a rubric for performance the class developed) to the first piece they recorded. She asks them to explain how practicing affected their performance. Most students are surprised by the extent to which practicing helped them improve their performance. Even though there are no prizes for practicing during the rest of the year, Ms. Raintree finds that most students continue to practice on a regular basis.

## Reinforcing Effort and Providing Recognition with Today's Learners

Blogs and other Web 2.0 tools provide opportunities to receive recognition from peers beyond the classroom in ways students have never had before. Today's tools make it possible for students to publish work in a variety of media formats, which can have a powerful impact on student motivation.

Although teacher feedback is still an absolute necessity, students often feel empowered when they see that their hard work is recognized and even used by an authentic audience.

One excellent example of how a teacher uses blogs, video conferencing, and wikis to provide recognition to his students is evident in Brian Crosby's TEDxDenverED speech, which he gave in June of 2010 during the ISTE conference in Denver, Colorado. In his speech, Brian explained how he uses a wide variety of online tools to connect his students to other students, teachers, and professionals. At one point, he talked about how his students used Skype to connect with another class in New Zealand to teach them how to do some of the science experiments they described in their blogs. With this activity, students reviewed their own learning and had the opportunity to be recognized as experts by peers on the other side of the world. You can view Brian's speech on YouTube, and you can also see samples of his students' work on his blog, "Learning is Messy."

## Tips for Teaching Using Reinforcing Effort and Providing Recognition

1. Ensure that your curriculum recognizes the importance of effort by allocating time over the course of the academic year to assist students in learning about effort and how to apply and track it. This means building attention to effort into curriculum documents and lesson design and delivery.
2. Reinforce what effort is and how knowledge about effort translates into success inside and beyond the classroom. This helps students develop a sense of control over their learning.
3. Keep praise simple and direct, using straightforward sentences without gushing or dramatizing.
4. Specify the particular accomplishment being praised, pointing out any noteworthy effort, care, or perseverance and calling attention to new skills or evidence of progress.
5. Vary the phrases you use to praise students, and use nonverbal communication along with praise to convey warmth and appreciation for students' efforts and achievements.

# 3

# Cooperative Learning

"An underlying purpose of cooperative learning is to make each group member a stronger individual in his or her own right."
> —David W. Johnson and Frank P. Johnson, *Joining Together*

In *The World is Flat*, Thomas Friedman states, "The best companies are the best collaborators. In the flat world, more business will be done through collaborations within and between companies, for a few simple reasons: The next layers of value creation, whether in technology, marketing, biomedicine, or manufacturing, are becoming so complex that no single firm or department is going to be able to master them alone" (2006, p. 439). In the layers of a complex world, the students of today need to possess not only intellectual capabilities but also the ability to function effectively in an environment that requires working with others to accomplish a variety of tasks.

Using cooperative learning helps teachers lay the foundation for student success in a world that depends on collaboration and cooperation. Few other instructional strategies are as theoretically grounded as cooperative learning (D. W. Johnson & R. T. Johnson, 2009), yet it is one of the most misunderstood practices found in classrooms (Antil, Jenkins, Wayne, & Vadasy, 1998; Koutselini, 2009).

Some of the confusion about cooperative learning stems from the different ways that people define it. For example, Drs. David Johnson and Roger Johnson (1999) use five elements to define cooperative learning: positive interdependence, face-to-face promotive interaction, individual and group accountability, interpersonal and small-group skills, and group processing (see Figure 3.1). Other researchers and practitioners define cooperative learning as a strategy that uses one or more of these elements, though generally not all five. For example, Kagan promotes the use of cooperative learning structures, highlighting positive interdependence and individual accountability (1985, 1990). Another model of cooperative learning, which is known as complex instruction, addresses positive interdependence, individual accountability, and group processing (Cohen, 1994). (For additional information about the various models of cooperative learning, see Aronson, Stephan, Stikes, Blaney, & Snapp, 1978; DeVries & Edwards, 1973; Howard, 1996; Sharan & Sharan, 1992; Slavin, 1978, 1983, 1990.)

## FIGURE 3.1
### Elements of the Cooperative Learning Model

| Element | Purpose | Instructional Implication |
|---|---|---|
| *Positive Interdependence* | Ensure that success by an individual promotes success among other group members. | Establish a cooperative goal structure and equally distribute resources. Help students develop a sense that they "sink or swim" together. |
| *Face-to-Face Promotive Interaction* | Individuals encourage and activate efforts to achieve and help one another learn. | Encourage discussion among group members and teach students about the importance of effort and how to provide others with recognition for their effort. |
| *Individual and Group Accountability* | Ensure that all members contribute to achievement of the goal and learn as individuals. | Establish an optimal group size and include individual assessments. Help students understand that each person needs to contribute to the success of the group. |
| *Interpersonal and Small-Group Skills* | Ensure that all members clearly understand effective group skills. | Provide initial and ongoing instruction on effective group skills such as communication, decision making, conflict resolution, leadership, and trust. |
| *Group Processing* | Promote group and individual reflection for maintenance of group effectiveness and success. | Establish dedicated time for group reflection by providing structures such as specific questions, learning logs, or sentence stems that focus on how well the team is functioning and how to function even better. |

Two of the five elements identified by Johnson & Johnson (1999) seem to be most essential for a learning activity to be considered a cooperative learning activity: positive interdependence and individual accountability. Without these elements, group learning structures can actually impede the learning process (Guerin, 1999; Ingham, Levinger, Graves, & Peckham, 1974; Latane, Williams, & Harkins, 1979).

Positive interdependence is a key element of cooperative learning because it emphasizes that everyone is in the effort together and that one person's success does not come at the expense of another's success. To foster positive interdependence, teachers must ensure that the workload of each individual is reasonably equal to the workload of other team members. Teachers can accomplish this by clearly defining roles and responsibilities during the cooperative learning activity.

The other key element of cooperative learning, individual accountability, refers to the need for each member of the team to receive feedback on how his or her personal efforts contribute to achievement of the overall goal. To ensure individual accountability, teachers can use formative and summative assessments to determine students' contributions to the group goal. This practice discourages the tendency for a few individuals to carry the workload of the group. In addition, individual accountability establishes a means by which each group member can demonstrate proficiency with regard to the knowledge and skills embedded within the goals of the cooperative learning activity.

## Why This Category Is Important

An instructional strategy for grouping students, cooperative learning provides opportunities for students to interact in ways that enhance and deepen their learning. This strategy is grounded in the theory that learning can be maximized through well-designed, intentional social interaction with others (Gerlach, 1994; Vygotsky, 1978). Cooperative learning provides an environment in which students can reflect upon their newly acquired knowledge, process what they are learning by talking with and actively listening to their peers, and develop a common understanding about various topics. As students talk through material, they arrive at a deeper understanding of it (Bandura,

2000). This process helps them retain what they learn. Cooperative learning also increases motivation for learning because students establish a sense of obligation to one another and a strong kinship with their peers that leads to greater buy-in, motivation, and increased achievement (Roseth, Johnson, & Johnson, 2008). Students develop a sense of positive interdependence—a "sink-or-swim-together" attitude whereby one student's success promotes success among others within the group. In addition, cooperative learning can improve cognitive and social aspects such as increased academic engagement, self-esteem, attitudes toward school, and opposition to social segregation and loneliness (Johnson, 1981; Johnson & Johnson, 2003, 2005; Morgan, Whorton, & Gunsalus, 2000).

To be included in McREL's 2010 study, cooperative learning structures had to feature at least positive interdependence and individual accountability. The average effect size of the 20 studies included in the 2010 analysis was 0.44. The overall effect size for studies included in the first edition of *Classroom Instruction That Works* was 0.73. Differences between the 2001 and the 2010 effect sizes may reflect the more stringent requirements for inclusion in the 2010 study.

Two of the studies reviewed for the 2010 analysis emphasize the importance of providing structure for student conversations that involve young students in cooperative learning (Souvignier & Kronenberger, 2007; Weiss, Kramarski, & Talis, 2006). For example, teachers might provide students with question stems (e.g., "Explain why . . ." "What is the difference between . . . and . . . ?") to help them provide explanations of their reasoning and to encourage elaboration of their explanations (Souvignier & Kronenberger, 2007). Teachers will need to model for students how to explain their reasoning and ask questions that encourage elaboration; they also need to provide opportunities for students to practice these skills so they can use them effectively in cooperative learning settings.

The cooperative learning task itself provides another form of structure that can encourage communication and mutual reasoning. Tasks should be interesting to students and present some cognitive conflict so students will need to talk about the task, sharing ideas and reasoning to resolve the conflict (Weiss et al., 2006). Strategies that promote elaboration are also effective for older students who will benefit from specific instruction in asking higher-order questions that help them rephrase information, make connections to existing knowledge, and provide examples during cooperative learning (Souvignier & Kronenberger, 2007).

## Classroom Practice for Cooperative Learning

Engaging students in cooperative learning is more than simply organizing them into groups. It requires careful planning before and intentional facilitation during cooperative learning activities. The recommended practices in this section help teachers think about the critical elements of cooperative learning, group size, and format as they plan group activities that support content learning and the development of collaboration skills.

We offer three recommendations for classroom practice that uses cooperative learning:

- Include elements of both positive interdependence and individual accountability.
- Keep group size small.
- Use cooperative learning consistently and systematically.

### Include elements of positive interdependence and individual accountability

When teachers employ cooperative learning as an instructional strategy, they offer students the opportunity to interact on a deep level. By intentionally incorporating the elements of positive interdependence and individual accountability, teachers set the stage for students to be responsible for their own learning; the learning of those in their group; and the ability to demonstrate what they know, understand, and are able to do. In the following example, note how the teacher carries out the two primary elements of positive interdependence and individual accountability.

### Example

Mr. Washington, a 5th grade social studies teacher, wishes to engage his students in a discussion about the events that led up to the American Revolution. At an earlier point in his career, he may have given a lecture on the topic and asked students to take notes, or he may have had students read the relevant chapter in the textbook and answer questions on an advance organizer. Recently, he and his colleagues read about how students learn through social interaction, so he's decided to try using a cooperative learning activity to get his students thinking about the conditions in Colonial America prior to 1760.

Mr. Washington begins the activity by emphasizing two important elements of cooperative learning: positive interdependence and individual accountability. He explains to students that everyone is responsible for his or her own learning and for contributing to the learning of all classmates. This means that each person will have a specific role in his or her group that will help the group accomplish the task. In addition, each person is responsible for making sure everyone else in his or her group can answer the important questions presented to the group.

Mr. Washington then explains the three roles in each group:

- One person reads the chapter aloud to the group.
- Another person takes notes that capture key ideas from the chapter.
- A third person asks group members a series of questions about the information and records the group's responses.

Mr. Washington designed these questions to assess student understanding and to provide opportunities for students to start thinking about events from various perspectives. He helps his students organize themselves into groups of three, and he allows students to self-select their specific roles within those groups. Once the groups are formed, they break into various work areas, expanding beyond the classroom. Each student has a netbook and is logged onto a service the class uses for collaborative note taking. As one student begins reading the chapter, a second student begins to type the key points. The students stop occasionally and discuss whether or not what was just read aloud was a key point. They also help one another decipher new vocabulary words and phrases. When they finish reading the chapter, the third student asks questions, which are provided by Mr. Washington, and records his peers' answers and the main discussion points on the group's collaborative document.

At the end of the session, Mr. Washington asks each group to pair with another group and compare the key points they identified from the chapter, along with their answers to his questions. He encourages them to write down any confusing points or questions they still have. The following day, he uses these collaborative documents to engage students in a discussion of the events that led up to the American Revolution, focusing on the differing perspectives held by colonists who advocated for independence and British citizens and loyalists.

Mr. Washington notices that his students' discussions and level of understanding are remarkably more sophisticated than they were in previous years. This is because students had an opportunity to grapple with the concepts during the previous day's small-group discussions and because they had more time to process their thinking (in ways that led to richer results than if students had independently completed a worksheet). To close the activity and address individual accountability, Mr. Washington asks every student to write a two- or three-paragraph summary that captures one of the two opposing perspectives of the period that were the subject of the class discussion.

## Keep group size small

Recommendations for organizing cooperative learning opportunities for students very often include limiting the group size to no more than five students per group (Lou et al., 1996). Studies show that as groups get larger, external and internal motivation tend to decrease, and members of larger groups tend to feel that their individual contributions will go unnoticed (Earley, 1989; McWhaw, Schnackenberg, Sclater, & Abrami, 2003; Sheppard & Taylor, 1999). Students are also less likely to experience social pressure for making contributions, which can motivate members of smaller groups. As the following example illustrates, larger group size may result in the loss of positive interdependence and erode individual accountability.

## Example

Ali and Jan are teaching partners who are committed to improving their instruction through peer observation. As Jan observes Ali's 8th grade science class, she notices that some students (who are working in cooperative groups of seven students each) are not fully engaged with the material or the activity. She also notes that one of the groups has subdivided into two self-selected smaller groups, and both of these smaller groups are now working more effectively than the larger group was before.

When Ali and Jan debrief the science lesson, Jan shares her observations about the cooperative groups and the student behavior in each group. Ali agrees that the size of the groups inhibited student participation and increased discipline issues. She also states that most students did not do as well as she had anticipated on the brief quiz she gave at the end of class. Ali determines that the larger group size inhibited participation and learning. During the next lesson, she reorganizes the groups so each is comprised of only four students.

## Use cooperative learning consistently and systematically

How often should you use cooperative learning? David Johnson and Frank Johnson argue that "any learning task in any subject area with any curriculum may be structured cooperatively" (2009, p. 476). They promote cooperative learning as the dominant approach in the classroom but also suggest that, as they develop expertise in using cooperative learning, teachers should integrate cooperative learning with competition and individual work. Other researchers suggest that grouping strategies are most effective when they are used at least once a week (Lou et al., 1996).

Some researchers caution teachers not to overuse cooperative learning activities (Anderson, Reder, & Simon, 1997). They remind educators that if students are expected to master skills and processes, they need independent practice for that learning to occur. This means teachers need to balance the use of cooperative learning with opportunities for students to practice skills and processes independently (Anderson, 2005; Rohrer & Taylor, 2007). Students might feel that cooperative learning is being overused, or they might become bored if they always work with the same group members or engage in the same type of cooperative learning group. Teachers can assign students to groups randomly or based on a variety of criteria (e.g., interests, birth month, colors they are wearing). To form groups easily, teachers can create or purchase grouping cards. Each deck includes a number of cards with the same design, and students form groups based on the cards they select. Teachers should limit the number of times they form cooperative groups based on ability (Lou et al., 1996). Grouping by ability can limit the knowledge and experience available to the group and lead to "group think." It can have negative effects on students' self-efficacy if they perceive that they have been placed in a group for which the teacher has low expectations (D. W. Johnson & F. P. Johnson, 2009). On a practical level, ability grouping does not reflect the world of work—students need experience working with people of varying interests, experiences, and abilities (Frey, Fisher, & Everlove, 2009).

Cooperative learning is a process. To support the success of cooperative learning, teachers must teach the steps of the process, provide students with opportunities to practice those steps, and clearly define the norms and parameters within which cooperative learning will take place (Tweed, 2009). Often, students are not used to assuming the various roles cooperative learning requires, and they do not have the group skills to make the most of the cooperative learning experience. As a result, it is important to provide opportunities for students to practice their roles and give appropriate feedback to other members of their group. Practicing these skills will enhance their interactions with peers and their academic success (Tomlinson, 2004).

To keep students' interest, teachers should vary the type of cooperative learning. Johnson and Johnson (2009) describe three types of cooperative learning groups: informal, formal, and base groups. Informal groups (e.g., pair-share, turn-to-your-neighbor) are ad hoc groups that last from a few minutes to an entire class period. They can be used to clarify expectations for tasks, focus students' attention, allow time for students to more deeply process information, or provide time for closure. Formal groups are designed to ensure that students have enough time to thoroughly complete an academic assignment; therefore, they may last for several days or even weeks. According to Johnson and Johnson (1999), tasks for these types of cooperative learning groups should include all five elements of cooperative learning. Base groups are long-term groups (e.g., for the semester or year) created to provide students with support over an extended period. These groups can be used to organize students and help them complete routine tasks, plan activities, have fun, and establish a general sense of belonging to the class. The example that follows illustrates how a teacher might use a formal cooperative learning group.

### Example

Ms. Sommerset's high school history class has been studying the role of propaganda during World War II. Students look at examples of how the right images, when combined with carefully chosen words, can send powerful messages that may or may not be completely factual. Ms. Sommerset gives an assignment to the class: Identify something in the classroom that is typically thought of as a rather benign, common item; then create a two-minute movie using images, background music, and messages that cast doubt upon or create fear about that item.

She divides the class into groups of four students, and each group has a graphics designer, writer, voice talent, and music talent. Using a digital video recorder and multimedia editing software, students take two class periods to conceptualize their ideas, write their scripts, create the graphics, and record the audio. Prior to starting the project, Ms. Sommerset allotted one class period to model how to use these tools.

At the end of the project, the groups watch one another's movies, noting with bemusement that, according to their projects, they should now fear pencils, laptops, spiral-bound notebooks, and cell phones. The teacher then uses these examples to have discussions about propaganda, political ads, and other messages that we see on television and in print. Through this cooperative learning task, students have a chance to interact and connect their ideas to see the power that multimedia can have, for better or for worse, over public opinion.

## Cooperative Learning with Today's Learners

Our classrooms are becoming increasingly diverse, not only culturally but also in terms of learning styles and levels of understanding (Antil et al., 1998; Garofano & Sable, 2008; Peterman, 2008). No one teacher can meet every need of every student, especially as we prepare students for a future of collaborating within a diverse workforce. Almost every model and iteration of what constitutes 21st century learning includes two concepts that have become keystones of preparing students for future endeavors: collaborating and creating. These skills are reflected in ISTE's NETS for students.

Using cooperative learning is one way that teachers can help students meet these standards. By helping students use a variety of media to produce nonlinguistic representations (e.g., drawings, audio, video, presentations) that demonstrate their learning and help them understand new concepts, teachers are tapping into a more creative method of working with content than simply memorizing information or completing a worksheet. Similarly, students can use digital environments to work with peers and create metaphors or analogies to show connections in their learning. In the process, they think creatively about the content outside the parameters of the particular unit of study.

Cooperative learning structures provide students with opportunities to be a viable part of a collaborative group, where they must work together with roles and deadlines as well as personalities and preferences. These skills are vital in today's learning and working environments, especially as those environments become increasingly diverse. An example of a project that exemplifies cooperative learning and the concepts outlined in the standards is the Flat Classroom Project. Cofounded by Vicki Davis of Westwood Schools in Camilla, Georgia, and Julie Lindsay of the Beijing International School in China, this project involves middle and high school students collaborating with peers around the world to identify key emerging technological and global trends. Students collaborate by video conferencing, blogging, posting their findings to a wiki, and sharing multimedia content. As a result, students learn how the ways they collaborate and communicate are affected by the very tools they are using for the project. Tied to Friedman's *The World is Flat*, students experience firsthand how open-source software, workflow software, and Voice over IP is, indeed, flattening the world, including their own classroom.

Now, more than ever, we have a plethora of tools that allow us to communicate and collaborate with peers, whether in our own workspace or on the other side of the world. Blogs allow students to share their thinking with a much broader audience than by simply handing assignments to teachers. Wikis serve as working documents and final showcases for cooperative learning projects. Social bookmarking helps students share and access resources as they work through a task together. Collaborative documents, such as Google Docs, allow students to collaborate in real time. When these tools are combined with well-defined cooperative learning projects, as in the previous U.S. History example, we give students powerful experiences in using Web 2.0 tools for authentic collaboration tasks. Studies show that well-organized cooperative learning opportunities positively affect academic as well as socioemotional achievement, self-esteem, motivation, and engagement with school, all while helping to minimize feelings of social isolation (Beesley & Apthorp, 2010).

We can no longer expect students to learn in isolation any more than we can expect to work in isolation. By giving students opportunities to learn and lead in cooperative groups, we are helping them develop those essential skills for higher education and the workplace.

## Tips for Teaching Using Cooperative Learning

1. Establish a classroom culture that supports cooperative learning by being clear with students about the norms and parameters within which cooperative learning will take place.
2. Focus on the underpinnings that lead to group success by establishing and teaching the structures and processes students will follow as they work in cooperative groups. Model what students should do as they move into and work in their cooperative groups. Be sure they understand how to use the social skills required of them.
3. Provide additional instruction, practice, and corrective feedback on the social skills necessary to function successfully in cooperative groups.

4. Ensure that the use of cooperative learning aligns with the intent for learning. When the target for learning includes mastery of skills or processes, balance the use of cooperative learning with sufficient opportunities for students to practice those skills and processes independently.

5. To avoid misuse of cooperative learning, use cooperative learning tasks that are well structured. A well-structured task has clearly defined goals for learning, roles, and responsibilities for each member, and it maintains individual accountability.

6. Design cooperative learning tasks to include strategic use of other instructional strategies that help students deepen their understanding and use knowledge meaningfully.

# Part II

## Helping Students
## Develop Understanding

# 4

# Cues, Questions, and Advance Organizers

"Questions that stretch students' minds, invite curiosity, provoke thinking, and instill a sense of wonder can keep students engaged."
—Chris Caram and Patsy Davis, *Inviting Student Engagement with Questioning*

Walk into any classroom and you probably won't have to wait very long before the teacher asks a question. Researchers have found that approximately 80 percent of teacher interactions with students involve cueing and questioning (Fillippone, 1998). A study conducted by McREL provides additional support for the claim that questioning is common in classrooms (Pitler & Hubbell, 2009). McREL analyzed data from 27,000 classroom observations conducted by principals and teachers in 24 states across the country using McREL's Power Walkthrough™ software. Data were gathered from teachers at all grade levels and in all types of districts (urban, suburban, rural). Observers noted cueing and questioning as the primary instructional strategies in 21 percent of the observations. Only the providing practice strategy was observed more frequently. Together, these were the primary strategies used in nearly half of all observations. It is clear from both research and classroom observations that the use of cues and questions is an important tool in teachers' tool belts. The other strategies in rank order were feedback, nonlinguistic representation, and setting objectives. Together, these accounted for about 40 percent of the observations.

We group cues and questions together in this category because they function in a similar manner; both activate students' prior knowledge and give them an idea of what they will learn. Cues are hints to students about the content of an upcoming lesson; they reinforce information that students already know and provide some new information on the topic. Similarly, questions allow students to access previously learned information on a topic and assess what they do not already know.

We also include advance organizers in this category because they help students use their background knowledge to learn new information. Advance organizers are stories, pictures, and other introductory materials that set the stage for learning. They are introduced before a lesson to draw attention to important points, identify relationships within the material, and relate material to students' prior knowledge (Bransford, Brown, & Cocking, 2000; Lefrancois, 1997; Mestre, 1994; Woolfolk, 2004). The most effective advance organizers provide an organized conceptual framework that is meaningful to the learner and allows the learner to relate concepts in the instructional material to elements of that framework (Martorella, 1991; White & Tisher, 1986).

Using cues, questions, and advance organizers at the beginning of a lesson or unit focuses learning on the important content to come. Such an approach can motivate students by tapping into their curiosity and interest in the topic. In addition, using higher-order questions can help students deepen their knowledge by requiring the use of critical-thinking skills (e.g., making inferences, analyzing perspectives).

This chapter emphasizes some specific practices that help teachers make the most effective use of cues, questions, and advance organizers to increase student understanding and achievement.

## Why This Category Is Important

How effective are cues, questions, and advance organizers in promoting student learning? To answer this question, McREL researchers calculated effect sizes for cues and questions (0.20) and advance organizers (0.74). The four studies related to advance organizers were analyzed separately because their use is associated with slightly different generalizations. The first edition of *Classroom Instruction That Works* reported a combined effect size of 0.59 for cues, questions, and advance organizers. The small effect size for cues and questions in the 2010 study may reflect the small number of studies (two) that met the criteria for inclusion. Although the effect size for questioning was small among the studies that McREL researchers reviewed, other recent meta-analyses report large effect sizes that support the use of questioning as an instructional strategy. Specifically, Schroeder, Scott, Tolson, Huang, and Lee (2007) found an effect size of 0.74 for questioning in science, and Sencibaugh (2007) reported an effect size of 1.18 for questioning in reading comprehension.

One of the studies related to cues and questions (Hay, Elias, Fielding-Barnsley, Homel, & Freiberg, 2007) in the 2010 analysis illustrates the effects of questioning on students with language difficulties. This study investigated teachers' use of four levels of questions, developed by Blank, Rose, and Berlin (2003), to enhance students' language development. Level 1 questions require students to name objects, events, topics, or concepts, a practice that increases their vocabulary. Level 2 questions focus on the organization and classification of the vocabulary, which helps students store and retrieve the information from memory. Level 3 questions require higher-order reasoning, helping students reorganize and elaborate on the information and link the new information to what they already know. Level 4 questions move to the abstract level and ask students to reflect on, restructure, and advance their perceptions about concepts. The results of this study indicate that systematic use of this tiered questioning strategy enhances students' vocabulary, their ability to organize information in verbal memory, and their ability to engage in verbal reasoning.

## Classroom Practice for Cues and Questions

Effective cues and questions help students access their prior knowledge and put that knowledge to use learning new information. There are four recommendations to help teachers fine tune their practice as they use cues and questions with their students:

- Focus on what is important.
- Use explicit cues.
- Ask inferential questions.
- Ask analytic questions.

## Focus on what is important

How do you decide which questions to ask to activate students' prior knowledge? You might be tempted to base your questions on some interesting aspect of the topic with the idea that something out of the ordinary will capture students' attention. Few would argue that we shouldn't make topics interesting to students, but if the goal is to help students achieve learning objectives, then it is critical for the questions you ask to address what is important to learn about a topic. If you do not focus on the important aspects of a topic, students might miss the point of the lesson or not understand how to integrate what you are teaching with their relevant prior knowledge.

### Example

Mr. Esperanza is beginning a unit on probability with his 10th grade mathematics class. To capture their attention and connect with their prior knowledge, he asks students how many people they think have won a million dollars in the state lottery. Some students make wild guesses, and others start talking about how they wish they could win a million dollars or what they would do if they won a million dollars. Mr. Esperanza quickly realizes that his question has not accomplished his purpose of focusing students on probability. He tries again by asking, "How do states determine the odds of someone winning the grand prize in the state lottery?" This prompts students to make comments about the odds of winning something and what they think that means. Mr. Esperanza builds on the students' comments and explains that during the unit on probability, they will learn how to weigh the possible outcomes of a decision by assigning probabilities to payoff values and finding expected values. He explains that this will help them make decisions such as whether they should purchase a high-deductible or low-deductible car insurance policy.

Mr. Esperanza learns a valuable lesson: to get the maximum benefit by using questions to help students access prior knowledge, choose questions carefully so that what you ask reminds students of what they know about a topic and keeps them focused on the objective.

## Use explicit cues

Sometimes the best approach is the direct one. Such is the case when you provide explicit cues that present students with a preview of to-be-learned information. Explicit cues activate students' prior knowledge by bringing to mind relevant personal experiences or situations that they encounter on a regular basis. They remind students of what they have already learned and help them build a framework for new learning. For example, a teacher might show students pictures that represent the causes of climate change and ask students to identify the causes about which they know the most and least. Other ways to provide explicit cues include telling students what to pay attention to as they read or view material, providing a list of questions that students will be able to answer as a result of a lesson, and discussing learning objectives for a lesson or unit (Valle & Callanan, 2006).

### Example

Mr. Frazier's high school government class is beginning a unit on the influence of science on federal policy. He shows his students a short segment from the documentary *An Inconvenient Truth* and tells them that during the unit they will discuss how such documentaries, along with other scientific information and data, influence public policy. He provides students with a list of questions that will help them summarize what they learn during the unit.

## Ask inferential questions

What is the capital of Kansas? Who wrote the Declaration of Independence? Questions such as these, which simply require students to recall information, are all too common in classrooms. When students access this "right there" information, they do not have to think deeply about what they know; consequently, such questions do not elicit much prior knowledge or help students create a sturdy framework for learning new information. When teachers ask questions that require students to make inferences, however, students draw upon what they already know to "fill in the blanks" and address missing information in the presented material. Teachers can help students make inferences about things, people, actions, events, or states of being (e.g., hypothermic, disenfranchised) by asking questions such as those in Figure 4.1.

FIGURE 4.1
Examples of Inferential Questions

| Events | Things/People | Actions | States of Being |
|---|---|---|---|
| • Who is usually involved in this event?<br>• During which season or time of the year does this event take place?<br>• Where does the event usually take place?<br>• What equipment is typically used in this event? | • What action is usually performed on this thing or person?<br>• How is this thing usually used?<br>• What is this thing part of?<br>• Does this thing have a particular taste, feel, smell, sound, color, number, or location? What is it?<br>• Does this thing have a particular value? | • Who or what usually performs this action?<br>• What effect does this action have on the taste, feel, sound, or look of a thing?<br>• How is the value of a thing changed by this action?<br>• How does this action change the size or shape of a thing? | • What is the basic process involved in reaching this state?<br>• What are some of the changes that occur when something reaches this state? |

## Example

To begin their study of impressionism, Ms. Rease's 8th grade art students view a number of examples of impressionist paintings and read about some artists who used the style. Ms. Rease knows that many students do not make the connection between art from a particular period and the social, political, or economic conditions of that time. To help students understand the relationship between art and other aspects of society, she asks her students to work in small groups and answer the following questions:

- How does impressionist art reflect the times in which it flourished?
- Why might impressionist art be popular today?

These questions help students fill in missing information about impressionism and better understand how it reflected and influenced society.

## Ask analytic questions

Analytic questions prompt students to think more deeply and critically about the information presented. Teachers can frame questions around the skills of analyzing errors, constructing support, and analyzing perspectives (Martorella, 1991; White & Tisher, 1986). Analyzing errors in thinking involves identifying and articulating when someone uses faulty logic, attacks a person rather than focuses on issues, uses weak references, confuses facts, or misapplies a concept. Constructing support involves providing support for an argument or proof for an assertion. Analyzing perspectives involves identifying and articulating personal perspectives about issues. Figure 4.2 presents examples of questions related to each of these skills. Such questions and skills require students to think at higher cognitive levels and allow students to make connections within the content.

FIGURE 4.2
Examples of Analytic Questions

| Analyzing Errors | Constructing Support | Analyzing Perspectives |
|---|---|---|
| • What are the errors in reasoning in this information?<br>• How is this information misleading?<br>• How could this information be corrected or improved? | • What is an argument that would support this claim?<br>• What are some of the limitations of this argument or the assumptions underlying it? | • Why would someone consider this to be good (or bad or neutral)?<br>• What is the reasoning behind this perspective?<br>• What is an alternative perspective, and what is the reasoning behind it? |

## Example

Ms. Tran is starting a writing project with her 4th grade students. She begins the lesson by explaining the objective for the project: We will be able to write persuasively. She also explains that students will write letters to their local city council representatives and ask them to put a school crossing light at the intersection of Main and Elm Streets because a teacher was recently injured while crossing the street there. Ms. Tran says, "We know that Ms. Dunlap's leg was broken when she was hit by a car two weeks ago, and we all agreed that a school crossing light might have prevented that accident. Before you start your prewriting, let's think about why some people might think it's a bad idea to put a crossing light at the intersection. If we are going to write a persuasive paper, we will have to take other people's perspectives into consideration. Let's start with a Venn diagram and put reasons the crossing light is a good idea in one circle and reasons the light might be considered a bad idea in the other. In the shared space, we will put ideas with which both groups of people can agree." By starting the lesson with an analytic question, Ms. Tran challenges her students to think at a higher cognitive level than if she had she simply said, "Today we are all going to write a letter telling the mayor that we want a school crossing light installed."

## Classroom Practice for Advance Organizers

There are four formats for advance organizers (expository, narrative, skimming, graphic) that help students improve their performance. As a general rule, using an expository advance organizer is a good choice, but which of the four formats is best depends on the material to be learned and the method of presentation. The recommendations for using advance organizers are based on the four different formats:

- Use expository advance organizers.
- Use narrative advance organizers.
- Use skimming as an advance organizer.
- Use graphic advance organizers.

### Use expository advance organizers

Expository advance organizers describe or explain in written or verbal form the new content students are about to learn, and they emphasize the important content. Expository advance organizers help students build a framework for learning by providing the meaning and purpose of what is to follow. They might also include more detail about or an example of what students will be learning. In some cases, an expository advance organizer might include text and pictures to provide additional clarification of complex information.

### Example

Ms. Holliman is teaching a lesson in nutrition and knows her 5th grade students have had some exposure to nutrition in 3rd grade. Before she begins the lesson with a short video on nutrition, she gives her students an anticipation guide to activiate their prior knowledge (see Figure 4.3). This anticipation guide also serves as a form of self-feedback for students following the video.

FIGURE 4.3

### Anticipation Guide

*Before we watch the video on nutrition, read each statement below and check one of the boxes to indicate whether you agree or disagree with the statement. After you watch the video, compare your opinions to the information presented in the video.*

| Statement | Me | Video |
|---|---|---|
| Children should have at least three servings of fruit each day. | ☐ Agree <br> ☐ Disagree | ☐ Agree <br> ☐ Disagree |
| We get all of our protein from meat and fish. | ☐ Agree <br> ☐ Disagree | ☐ Agree <br> ☐ Disagree |
| Some people are allergic to milk products. | ☐ Agree <br> ☐ Disagree | ☐ Agree <br> ☐ Disagree |

## Use narrative advance organizers

Narrative advance organizers present information to students in a story format. This type of advance organizer serves to engage students' interest while at the same time activating their prior knowledge on a topic. Narrative advance organizers can take a variety of forms. The teacher might read a short story from the time period students are about to explore, play a video clip to introduce the key vocabulary of the upcoming unit, or even tell a personal story.

## Example

Before teaching his students the formula for calculating the area of an irregular trapezoid, Mr. Silverman tells his students about the time he and his wife built a stone patio in their backyard. Before going to the store, he had to determine how much stone to buy. He wanted to make sure he didn't buy too much stone and waste money or buy too little and have to make several trips to the store for more supplies. He explains how he measured the area for the patio, draws illustrations on the board, and demonstrates how he was able to come up with exactly the right amount of stone he needed.

This narrative advance organizer gives Mr. Silverman's students a focus on why learning how to calculate the area of an irregular trapezoid is something that has importance outside of the classroom. It helps set the objective more clearly, and it provides his students with a concrete example they can then use to build meaning.

## Use skimming as an advance organizer

Skimming is the process of quickly looking over material to get a general impression before reading it fully. Some teachers don't think about skimming as an advance organizer, but it can be a very powerful tool. Done appropriately, it helps students create a picture of what the material addresses, and it helps organize the new information. Providing questions to guide the skimming process helps students access prior knowledge that is relevant to the new information. Done prior to instruction, this gives students a conceptual framework upon which they can build new learning.

Block, Gambrell, and Pressley (2002) refer to skimming as "tilling the text." To "till the text," students read all subheads and points of emphasis, note the level of density of ideas, and note content flow. This helps them identify key points, allows them to slow down when they come across something they find intriguing, and encourages them to make predictions about what they are about to learn. Another strategy that involves skimming is "scamper and scan." With this strategy, teachers encourage students to quickly skim or "scamper" through a nonfiction text and then decide which section they want to read first, scanning closely for specific information of interest (Lapp, 2004). Both of these processes improve student understanding and motivation to read.

## Example

Mr. Chung decides that asking his chemistry class to skim the next chapter is a good way for students to quickly get a sense of the content they will soon study. He provides his students with some questions to guide their skimming:

- Based on the title of this chapter and what you already know, what do you predict will be included in this chapter?
- What is the flow of the content of this chapter?
- What are the major ideas in this chapter?
- What do the pictures tell you about the content of this chapter?

After students finish skimming the chapter, Mr. Chung asks them to pair up with classmates and share one idea from the chapter they already knew and one idea they are looking forward to learning.

## Use graphic advance organizers

What is the difference between a graphic organizer and a graphic advance organizer? Timing and intent. Teachers provide students with graphic advance organizers in advance of the learning to introduce them to new material. To be effective, graphic advance organizers must clearly communicate what students are expected to learn (Ausubel, 1960).

## Example

Ms. Allison's 3rd grade class is starting a unit in music class about the various families of the orchestra. Ms. Allison gives her students an advance organizer that shows the four instrument families they are going to discuss (see Downloadable Figure 2). As each family is presented, her students add examples to each of the circles: "Members of the family," "How sound is produced," and "Outside the orchestra." This intentional use of an advance organizer gives Ms. Allison's students a clear understanding of the expectations for learning and what will be assessed.

## Using Cues, Questions, and Advance Organizers with Today's Learners

In addition to the many dynamic traditional tools that teachers can use as advance organizers—demonstrations, video clips, drawings, graphics, and skimming—online and multimedia tools give teachers even more ways to engage students in new content, activate background knowledge, and scaffold learning. These tools can include creating graphic organizers with brainstorming software, accessing videos online, listening to audio clips, and playing interactive games. For example, a teacher can briefly introduce the parts of the cell as the class begins a unit on the structure and function of cells and organisms. Then, to further engage students in the new content, the teacher can direct students to a reputable and safe website where an interactive model of a cell reinforces the material and engages students in novel ways. In this way, interactive multimedia is used as an engaging introduction to content that will also be taught by more traditional methods. The teacher could also have students watch a BrainPOP movie about cells and cell structures or play an interactive game about cell structure online. If the teacher saved this interactive experience for the end of the unit, students would have been less enthusiastic about these simple introductory activities.

The web is full of short video clips and interactive media that engage students and help to introduce new content. Too often, however, these tools are used toward the end of a unit as "extras." They can be much more powerful if they are used at the beginning of a unit as advance organizers, just as short stories or picture books have traditionally been used to introduce topics and ideas. Everything from bridge types to percentages to writing transitions can be introduced with an engaging video, interactive, or quiz.

## Tips for Teaching Using Cues, Questions, and Advance Organizers

1. As you introduce a unit or lesson, there is no need to be subtle or ambiguous with students about what you want them to learn. Use explicit cues to tell students what they are about to learn, and help them identify and discuss what they already know about the topic.

2. Make it easy for students to access their prior knowledge by providing explicit cues in a variety of formats, including questions that guide their listening, reading, or viewing of information about a topic.

3. The more students know about a topic, the more interested they will be in it. Asking questions or providing cues that help students access their prior knowledge about a topic brings that knowledge to the conscious level and increases the likelihood that students will pay attention to or engage with new information related to the topic.

4. It is sometimes difficult to think of good inferential or analytic questions "in the moment" while you are teaching. Plan for the use of inferential and analytic questions by creating a list of relevant and useful questions before you begin a lesson or unit.

5. Keep a list of possible inferential and analytic questions (such as the ones on pages 55 and 56) readily accessible (e.g., on your desk, near the board, in your lesson plan book) to remind you to use such questions on a regular basis.

6. Use a variety of graphic organizers to help students access their prior knowledge, but keep in mind that the purpose of graphic organizers is to make clear to students what they will be learning with regard to a particular topic. Ensure that the connection between the graphic organizer and the focus of the lesson is clear.

# 5

# Nonlinguistic Representations

"Image and other nonlinguistic modes take on specific roles in the construction of school knowledge."
—Carey Jewitt, *Multimodality and Literacy in School Classrooms*

Mr. Cho asked his class to pay close attention to what occurred in their minds as they read about Rosa Parks refusing to move to a seat in the rear of the bus. Tad explained that he pictured himself sitting on the bus, watching people and listening to their reactions. Kaitlin said that she was moved by the emotions she felt as she pictured Mrs. Parks standing up for her beliefs. These students experienced the transformation that can occur when one's mind quickly changes linguistic information into a nonlinguistic mental image. We don't see words in a literal sense, but we do create the mental images that allow us to experience emotions, sights, sounds, tastes, and tactile experiences.

Psychologists believe that information is stored in memory in two ways: as words (linguistic) and as images (nonlinguistic). This chapter focuses on the imagery form (Clark & Paivio, 1991; Paivio, 2006). Imagery is expressed as mental pictures or physical sensations, such as smell, taste, touch, kinesthetic association, and sound (Richardson, 1983). Such nonlinguistic representations provide students with useful tools that merge knowledge presented in the classroom with mechanisms for understanding and remembering that knowledge (Jewitt, 2008; Kress, 1997).

In this chapter, we discuss five nonlinguistic representation strategies teachers can use to encourage students to create, store, and manipulate information either mentally or with concrete tools and displays. These include

- Creating Graphic Organizers: Students combine words and phrases with symbols, arrows, and shapes to represent relationships in the knowledge being learned. Graphic organizers include representations for descriptive patterns, time-sequence patterns, process patterns, episode patterns, generalization patterns, and concept patterns.
- Making Physical Models/Manipulatives: Students are involved in hands-on tasks to create concrete representations of knowledge.
- Generating Mental Pictures: Students visualize the knowledge. Mental pictures incorporate senses, physical sensations, and emotions.
- Creating Pictures, Illustrations, and Pictographs: Students draw, paint, or use technology to create symbolic pictures that represent knowledge being learned.
- Engaging in Kinesthetic Activity: Students engage in physical movement associated with specific knowledge to generate a mental image of content and skills being learned.

## Why This Category Is Important

When teachers use nonlinguistic representation strategies, they help students represent knowledge as imagery. These strategies are powerful because they tap into students' natural tendency for visual image processing, which helps them construct meaning of relevant content and skills and have a better capacity to recall it later (Medina, 2008). For example, diagrams and models are used in mathematics and science to help represent phenomena that students cannot observe, such as the arrangement of atoms in a molecule and how that arrangement changes during a chemical reaction (Michalchik, Rosenquist, Kozma, Kreikemeier, & Schank, 2008). In other subjects, students can use nonlinguistic representations such as graphic organizers to organize information into a conceptual framework. Using this type of representation increases transfer of knowledge because it allows students to see how the information connects in new situations (Bransford, Brown, Cocking, 1999). The ultimate goal for using these strategies is to produce nonlinguistic representations of knowledge in the minds of students so they are better able to process, organize, and retrieve information from memory.

Recent research continues to support the recommendation that teachers explicitly teach students how to use nonlinguistic representations and promote the use of these strategies as a way for students to enhance their learning and achievement. McREL's 2010 analysis of the relevant research on nonlinguistic representations found an overall positive effect size of 0.49 for this category of strategies. This represents an average gain in achievement of approximately 19 percentile points. The original *Classroom Instruction That Works* reported an overall effect size of 0.75 for this category. The lower effect size for the 2010 study could reflect the small number of studies or another aspect of the study's methodology (e.g., analytic models, statistical adjustments). Studies in the 2010 analysis indicated that the impact of using nonlinguistic representations can multiply when teachers and students use the strategy in combination with other strategies (Beesley & Apthorp, 2010). For example, graphic organizers can be used as a tool for summarizing and identifying similarities and differences. They also can be used as advance organizers and for representing learning from generating and testing hypotheses.

Two studies from the 2010 analysis illustrate this point. One of these studies examined the use of software that creates an interactive computer environment with graphing calculator functionality to help low-achieving 11th grade students understand quadratic functions (Bos, 2007). Students changed values with a slider or in an interactive math box to manipulate an interactive graph and table. This experimentation helped students find predictable patterns for the graphs. They applied the patterns as they made and tested conjectures to solve problems. Students who used this software outperformed students in a control group (who didn't use the software) on a standardized test of quadratic functions. In another study, students in a foreign language class (German 1) learned vocabulary in context by working in cooperative groups to create a fashion show skit that incorporated clothing-related vocabulary (Sildus, 2006). Each student took on two roles (announcer and model) during the skit. When compared with students in the control group who were involved in more traditional activities, such as completing worksheets and answering short response questions, this kinesthetic activity helped students in the experimental group make greater achievement gains. The adjusted average post-test score for the experimental group was 19.57 versus 17.03 for the control group. (The scores were adjusted to account for differences between the groups before the intervention.)

## Classroom Practice for Nonlinguistic Representations

There are a variety of ways that teachers can help students generate nonlinguistic representations of knowledge, and students will benefit most when teachers structure learning activities that use the range of nonlinguistic representations we previously described. The classroom practices described in this section emphasize that when they engage in nonlinguistic representation, students elaborate on or add to their existing knowledge. For example, a student elaborates on her knowledge when she creates a physical model to represent division of mixed numbers. This is one reason that nonlinguistic representation is an effective strategy; the elaboration of knowledge that results from nonlinguistic representation helps students understand knowledge at a deeper level and recall it much more easily. In addition, when students explain and justify their nonlinguistic representations, they enhance the power of elaboration.

There are five recommendations for classroom practice with nonlinguistic representations. Teachers should provide opportunities for students to

- Use graphic organizers.
- Make physical models or manipulatives.
- Generate mental pictures.
- Create pictures, illustrations, and pictographs.
- Engage in kinesthetic activities.

### Use graphic organizers

Graphic organizers combine linguistic and nonlinguistic forms of information. In other words, as students create or complete graphic organizers, they use both words and symbols to represent and organize knowledge. To help students take advantage of the power of graphic organizers, teachers should provide them with information about and opportunities to use graphic organizers when developing summaries, taking notes, identifying similarities and differences, generating and testing hypotheses, and organizing information that may be difficult or poorly organized (Lehrer & Chazen, 1998; National Council of Teachers of Mathematics, 2000).

Six types of graphic organizers are commonly used in the classroom to organize information: Descriptive, Time Sequence, Process/Cause-Effect, Episode, Generalization/Principle, and Concept (see Downloadable Figure 3). It is important to explicitly teach students how to use these tools. As with any type of procedural knowledge, introduce the graphic organizer with familiar content so students can focus on learning to use the graphic organizer without having to worry about new content (Anderson, 1995; Karpicke & Roediger, 2008; Newell & Rosenbloom, 1981).

## Example

Ms. Aragon's 8th grade class is studying the relationship between the social environment and science research. Ms. Aragon provides her students with a graphic organizer that states the generalization "A country's social environment greatly impacts the quality and quantity of science research that it can support." She then provides several examples, such as "A country with political unrest may not be able to provide an environment conducive to scientific research" or "Scientists fearing religious or political persecution may not feel free to conduct experiments or share their findings freely." She asks students to work in pairs to select one of the examples and complete a time sequence that depicts significant events related to the example. Students are allowed to use the Internet or other resources available in the classroom to find information related to the example they select.

Miguel and Maurice select the development of the polio vaccine, and they create a related time sequence graphic organizer. They volunteer to share their time line with the class, explaining why they included each event and how placing the events along the time line helped them understand how social environment influences science research. After Miguel and Maurice present their time line to the class, Ms. Aragon asks if anyone has questions for them. Angelina asks Miguel and Maurice why they hadn't included the research that Dr. Albert Sabin was conducting during the same time. She and Violet had selected the same example and thought his work was significant because it led to another way to fight polio, and there was some controversy between people who supported Salk's work and people who supported Sabin's work. Maurice responds and says that he and Miguel hadn't thought about it that way, but he recognizes the point that Angelina is making. After several other groups present their time lines, Ms. Aragon gives her students three minutes to write a two-sentence summary of key points about the generalization and the example they selected.

## Make physical models or manipulatives

Physical models are concrete representations of academic content or concepts. Generating or manipulating such representations helps students create mental images of the relevant knowledge. The most difficult task for teachers often lies in making sure that students glean the appropriate information from the experience of creating or using physical models. Many times, students are so enamored with the materials and the experience of manipulating the concrete pieces that paying attention to the content or concepts they need to learn becomes secondary. Therefore, teachers must carefully examine their learning activities to ensure that students are both engaged in the process of making and using physical models and engaged with the specifics of the targeted knowledge.

### Example

Mr. Teal's 3rd graders are beginning to explore fractions. Mr. Teal starts by asking them to solve a problem: Six children are sharing 14 cookies so that each child gets the same number of cookies. How many cookies can one child have? The students have a number of tools available to help them solve the problem and represent their solutions (e.g., linking cubes, paper and pencils for drawing). During the first lesson, Mr. Teal is able to observe the different ways that students think about fractions. After a few more lessons, students solve more problems and begin to develop a deeper understanding of fractions.

Mr. Teal then introduces fraction circles, which are circles cut into a different number of total pieces (see Figure 5.1), and he begins with some simple tasks. He asks students to use fraction circles to decide which is larger: $\frac{1}{5}$ or $\frac{1}{8}$. After students have some experience with similar problems, they begin to recognize that larger denominators translate into more (and smaller) pieces. Eventually, Mr. Teal thinks his students are ready to explore the idea of comparing fractions a little further. He asks his students to use fraction circles to decide which is larger: $\frac{5}{8}$ or $\frac{8}{10}$.

Maria and Tyler decide to use circles with eight and ten pieces. They lay five of the pieces from the "eight circle" next to eight pieces of the "ten circle" to see which is larger. As a result, they notice that the eight pieces from the "ten circle" leave less of the original circle visible. Using this method, they conclude that $\frac{8}{10}$ is larger than $\frac{5}{8}$.

FIGURE 5.1
Example of Fraction Circles

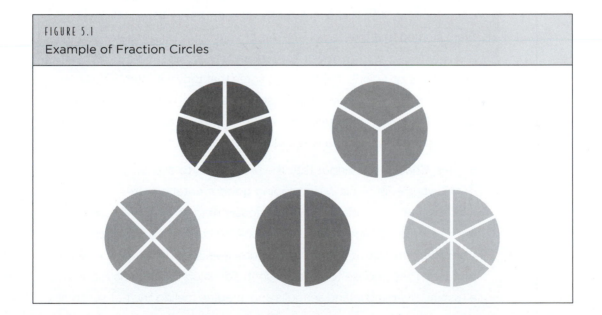

## Generate mental pictures

As students are presented with new information, the most direct way for them to generate a nonlinguistic representation is to create a mental picture of that information. This helps them make sense of the information and store their learning for future use. Teachers can facilitate students' construction of mental pictures by providing details that enable students to incorporate sounds, smells, tastes, and visual details as part of the overall mental picture. For abstract concepts, teachers might need to model the process several times, since it is difficult to create a mental picture that is highly symbolic. When teachers provide experiences for concrete and abstract concepts, students become better equipped to use this powerful strategy on their own. Forming a mental picture is often a good first step to understanding new information. With a mental picture as the foundation, students can use another nonlinguistic strategy to develop a deeper understanding of the relevant knowledge.

## Example

Ms. Chacon and Ms. Gleason, two 5th grade teachers, are planning their next unit of language arts instruction. As the teachers work together, they discuss how students in previous years struggled with the unit on poetry. Ms. Gleason recently attended a professional development session that focused on the use of nonlinguistic representations as a way to improve student learning, enhance retention, and extend learning to other situations. The teachers agree that they will intentionally use three nonlinguistic representation strategies (using graphic organizers, generating mental pictures, and creating pictures) as often as possible in the upcoming unit as a way to strengthen student learning.

Ms. Chacon points out that the first step is to explicitly teach students what is involved in developing good mental pictures. She finds a poem that her students have previously read so they will work with familiar material. Next, the teachers look for items from the poem they want to emphasize as they help students develop skills related to mental pictures. They choose to have students focus on the sounds made by a rushing river and inland seagulls and imagine feeling the hot summer sun beating down on their skin. Finally, they encourage students to consider the events of the poem and picture a boy's face when he sees a large salmon leap out of the river and into the air.

Ms. Gleason uses two graphic organizers to help students make sense of the poems they read and remember the vocabulary. She selects the concept map to organize ideas and information along with the Frayer Model to teach and reinforce new vocabulary words (see Downloadable Figures 4 and 5). In addition, the teachers agree that every time they ask students to create a mental picture that represents an important part of a poem, they will also ask students to develop a picture that captures the essence of the concept they are learning. Finally, the teachers ask students to create pictures for each of the new vocabulary words and add those pictures next to the appropriate definitions in their vocabulary notebooks. This application of multiple nonlinguistic representation strategies helps students solidify their learning.

## Create pictures, illustrations, and pictographs

Most students have drawn or colored pictures that represent knowledge. Students might be less familiar with pictographs, however, which use symbols or symbolic pictures to represent information. Pictures and pictographs provide opportunities for students to represent their learning in a personalized manner. Creating pictures (especially by hand or on a computer) that are personally meaningful can be especially helpful when students are learning new vocabulary words and terms. Technology provides a way to add animation to pictures, which enhances the effect of using pictures to represent knowledge (Höffler & Leutner, 2007).

### Example

Ms. Luis, a 2nd grade teacher, has been implementing literature circles throughout the school year, but she recently noticed that her students are tiring of the routine. She wants to find a way to engage students in discussions of the books they are reading in a format other than the oft-used face-to-face discussions or journaling. She also noticed that many students seem to gravitate toward the pictures, animations, and recorded audio they have encountered via several software suites on the class computer. She often finds students replaying segments when they learn new or confusing skills and content. Therefore, she wonders if she could tap into this interest to make her literature circles more engaging.

She decides to try VoiceThread, a collaborative online resource that allows users to upload pictures, videos, or documents, which then benefit from "group conversations" in the form of text comments, recorded audio, or video. This software also allows users to "doodle" on the uploaded files in order to highlight a particular point or make a quick sketch of an idea. All of these contributions to the group conversation are shared among all students and help to engage students during the learning and sharing processes.

Ms. Luis then introduces VoiceThread and its capabilities to her students. She helps them navigate to the website, create their own "identities," and upload images they want to use for their avatars. This activity presents a perfect opportunity to discuss online safety and why students should not use personal photographs of themselves. (Many students choose to use animals or favorite cartoon characters as their avatars.) They also practice recording their voices and drawing with the mouse, both of which require fine motor practice.

During the next literature circle, Ms. Luis pairs students for the activity. During the first half-hour, the class reads two folk tales together. Ms. Luis asks her students what they think makes a story a folk tale. After gathering a few initial ideas, Ms. Luis directs them to a drawing program on the computer. Each pair considers the qualities and attributes associated with folk tales and then creates an appropriate drawing. One pair, for example, points out that although characters in folk tales do not necessarily have magical abilities, they often have superhuman qualities, such as being very large or able to create something very quickly. They then draw a picture of Paul Bunyan and his blue ox.

After class, Ms. Luis uploads all of the drawings to VoiceThread. She then directs students to record their voices along with their pictures. In this way, students can add to their growing knowledge of folk and fairy tales. They are likewise able to listen to their peers explain their own nonlinguistic representations. Over the next few weeks, students add to their folk tale definitions by creating more nonlinguistic representations and recording their thoughts. Revisiting the many comments on

VoiceThread reinforces learning for students and reenergizes Ms. Luis's literature circles. At the end of the unit, Ms. Luis archives this material as part of each student's digital portfolio.

## Engage in kinesthetic activities

As students engage in physical movement associated with specific knowledge, they generate a mental image of that knowledge. This is true because mental images include physical sensations. When students move around as part of learning activities, they create more neural networks in their brains and the learning stays with them longer (Jensen, 2001). Kinesthetic activities include roleplaying, acting out vocabulary words, and using one's body to illustrate concepts. For example, students can arrange cards representing sentence parts on the classroom floor (King & Gurian, 2006), tap out the rhythm of poems and rhymes to create awareness of the rhythm of language (Pica, 2010), or use hand gestures to cue their memory of comprehension strategies (predict, question, clarify, and summarize). The gestures help students remember what the strategy is and how, when, and why to use it when reading (International Reading Association, 2010). Students can use their bodies to demonstrate their understanding of the motions of objects (e.g., planets orbiting the sun). As they make the motions (or take different physical perspectives) and talk about what they are doing, they encode information in their memory in multiple ways, helping them increase their understanding of concepts (Plummer, 2009).

### Example #1

Mr. Teague's 9th grade world history class is studying imperialism. From past experience, he knows that students often struggle to understand all the facets of this concept. Mr. Teague recently saw a video on TeacherTube that demonstrates how another teacher uses physical movement in his science class to help students understand concepts, and he thinks it is worth a try in his class. He begins by projecting an image of a graphic organizer that depicts key characteristics of imperialism along with some examples. He then asks students to work in small groups to decide how they would demonstrate some of the characteristics of imperialism or use their bodies to illustrate the concept. He tells them they can add sounds, pictures, or music to their demonstrations if they think it will help their classmates form a more complete mental image of the concept.

Talia, Juan, and Ellen decide to focus their demonstration on the power aspect of imperialism and show how that played out politically, economically, and culturally. They then develop three short skits that focus on imperialism in Africa. One skit depicts British archeologists who find ancient treasures in Egypt and send them to the British Museum for display. A second skit shows how aristocrats would go on safari, hunt wild animals for their pelts, and return with what were deemed exotic gifts at the time. A third skit shows Britain's role in building the Suez Canal. After each group presents its demonstration, Mr. Teague asks his students to write in their journals about what they now understand about imperialism and how the kinesthetic activity helped them develop this understanding.

## Example #2

Ms. Schaffer wants her students to develop an understanding of the words they encounter in her 7th grade language arts class. As students read various short stories, they are asked to enter the words they don't understand on an interactive whiteboard at the front of the class. After all of the words are entered, Ms. Schaffer asks her students to devise ways that would help them remember the words. Several students respond by asking if it would be okay to demonstrate the meanings by acting out the words. The students self-select into pairs and come up with unique ways to demonstrate their words. Mitch and Heather decide to hide under their desks and then come out to demonstrate the word *emerge.* Sandy and T. J. demonstrate the word *defenestrate* by pretending to throw different objects out of a window. Sarah and Matt struggle with their word, *antipodes*, but after a few attempts, they agree to stand at different ends of the classroom to symbolize being on the direct opposite side of something. As each team demonstrates the meaning of the word selected, other students are asked to mimic the actions. When all teams finish representing their words, Ms. Schaffer asks students to share positive thoughts about the learning experience. Almost all of her students respond that they have a better understanding of the vocabulary words because they were actively engaged, and the movement helped them remember the meanings.

## Nonlinguistic Representations with Today's Learners

With the plethora of tools that allow today's learners to create drawings, movies, animations, music, and podcasts, it is little wonder that many researchers postulate that we are quickly moving beyond a text-based society to one in which all forms of communication have equal value (Lucas, 2005; Pink, 2005; Prensky, 2001; Reynolds, 2008). This position argues that we need to know how to communicate effectively by writing for a variety of audiences and that this ability—to effectively communicate through visual and audio media—is becoming an expectation in nearly all realms of life.

For example, imagine that two high school students are asked to give a three-minute speech and persuasively argue opposing viewpoints of a current issue. One student prepares a PowerPoint presentation with only a few pictures and slides of text, which he reads verbatim to the audience. The second student prepares a short video with limited text, compelling background music, and powerful images that illustrate key points of his argument. Though both students have valid arguments, the second student is able to tap into the interests and emotions of his audience and help them construct mental images, making his viewpoints better understood and more memorable than the first student's.

With each passing day, it is easier to assume that our students will need communication skills far beyond the basic ability to convey ideas with the written word. Teachers, therefore, must be cognizant of how they model the use of images, video, music, and sounds to convey information in ways that increase understanding. In this way, teachers not only provide good examples for 21st century learners but also leverage the power of nonlinguistic representation for making sense of new information.

## Tips for Teaching Using Nonlinguistic Representations

1. Model the use of the strategies for nonlinguistic representation through demonstrations and think-alouds.
2. Provide students with opportunities to practice each of the strategies with familiar information before they are expected to use the strategies with new material. This makes it possible for students to focus on the process and not worry about learning new content at the same time.
3. Provide students with a variety of opportunities to use nonlinguistic representations as they learn new content.
4. Model how students can use more than one nonlinguistic representation as they learn a new concept or vocabulary term. For example, students can create a mental picture of an action word and then demonstrate the appropriate action.
5. Provide students with information about and opportunities to use graphic organizers when developing summaries, taking notes, identifying similarities and differences, generating and testing hypotheses, and organizing information that may be difficult or poorly organized.

# 6

# Summarizing and Note Taking

"Very few students are taught even basic 'note taking' skills . . . despite the fact that students are expected to take extensive notes . . . and despite the recognized usefulness of note taking for storing, learning, and thinking about what is being taught."

—Françoise Boch and Annie Piolat, *Note Taking and Learning: A Summary of Research*

Harvey, a freshman at a large state university, walks into the first class of his college career: English 101. It's a huge auditorium with rows of seats that lead down to a podium and screen at the front of the room. He looks around as other students enter and is relieved to see several new acquaintances from his dorm. They sit near him and start taking out the various tools they will use to take notes during the lecture. Though the setting is very different from his small, rural high school, Harvey knows that his ability to capture key ideas in his notes will serve him as well in this environment as it did throughout his high school years. As class begins, he uses his laptop to type quick, informal outlines that capture what the professor is saying. As he goes, he summarizes salient points at the end of each section with one or two highlighted sentences.

"Wow," says Alicia, one of the girls from his dorm, as she looks over at his screen. "You take really good notes." Harvey looks over at her laptop and sees that Alicia had at first tried to type every word the professor was saying. Later, she became fatigued and barely managed to capture even keywords from the lecture. Harvey looks back at his screen and begins to wonder when and how he learned to take good notes. Which teacher or teachers had taught him this particular skill?

The strategies of summarizing and note taking facilitate learning by providing opportunities for students to capture, organize, and reflect on important facts, concepts, ideas, and processes they will need to access at a later time (Piolat, Olive, & Kellogg, 2005). When students summarize, they must sort, select, and combine information, which can lead to increased comprehension (Boch & Piolat, 2005). Note taking, like summarizing, requires students to identify essential information. When students take notes, they must access, sort, and code information, which can help them memorize information and conceptualize new ideas. We include summarizing and note taking in the same category because they both require students to distill information into a parsimonious and synthesized form.

## Why This Category Is Important

Summarizing is the process of distilling information down to its most salient points to aid in understanding, memorizing, and learning the relevant material. Similarly, note taking refers to the process of capturing key ideas—through writing, drawing, or audio recording—for later access. Summarizing and note taking help students deepen their understanding of information because these strategies involve higher-order thinking skills. Students must analyze information at a deep level as they decide which information to keep, which to delete, and which to replace with more general terms (Anderson, & Hidi, 1988/1989; Broer, Aarnoutse, Kieviet, & van Leeuwe, 2002; Hidi & Anderson, 1987). For example, a student is reading about the subphylum vertebrata and learns that this group of animals includes jawless fish, bony fish, sharks, rays, amphibians, reptiles, mammals, and birds. In order to simplify the definition, the student combines "jawless fish" and "bony fish" and simply says "most fish."

Medina (2008) provides further support for the relationship among summarizing, note taking, and higher-order thinking skills. In *Brain Rules*, he identifies 12 principles that characterize how our brain works. Many of these principles have connections to summarizing and note taking, including the importance of repeating information (by summarizing or rereading notes) and recording information with pictures (a form of note taking).

Findings from McREL's 2010 study indicate that summarizing and note taking have positive effects across content areas and grade levels, with note taking having a significantly higher impact on learning than summarizing does (effect sizes 0.90 and 0.32, respectively). The effect size for note taking (0.90) is similar to the overall combined effect size (1.00) for summarizing and note taking that was reported in the first edition of this book. Seven studies related to note taking and 10 studies related to summarizing were included in the 2010 report. These studies indicate that students who employ summarizing and note-taking strategies consistently perform better on academic assessments than do students in control groups who do not use these techniques.

Engaging students in generic summarizing strategies as a way to review information is more effective at improving academic performance than no review, but it is not as effective as structured summarizing strategies (Kobayashi, 2006). Evidence indicates that summarizing alone is not the most effective technique for improving student achievement (Takala, 2006). Teachers might achieve better results if they teach students to use summarizing in conjunction with other cognitive strategies. For example, Hattie and Timperley (2007) report an effect size of 0.86 for reciprocal teaching, which includes summarizing, questioning, clarifying, and predicting.

The research literature on note taking (e.g., Boch & Piolat, 2005; Makany, Kemp, & Dror, 2009) highlights the idea that no single form of note taking is correct. Students benefit from using a variety of formats for taking notes. Research describes both linear formats, such as outlining, and nonlinear formats, such as webbing or mapping (Robinson, Katayama, Dubois, & Devaney, 1998). Evidence is mixed with regard to whether linear note taking formats are more effective than nonlinear formats.

Evidence from the 2010 study also suggests that note-taking strategies are not intuitive; this means that students benefit from explicit instruction in note-taking strategies, particularly those that are guided and more structured (Hamilton, Seibert, Gardner, & Talbert-Johnson, 2000; Patterson, 2005). For example, in the study conducted by Hamilton and colleagues, teachers provided students with structured notes that consisted of sentences and facts with important information or words omitted. Students filled in these blanks as they progressed through instruction and as a result showed improved performance on classroom quizzes.

## Classroom Practice for Summarizing

When we teach students to write, we encourage them to add details and use descriptive language, adding colorful adjectives and adverbs so the reader can more easily visualize and understand what the writer is saying. Conversely, when we teach students to summarize, we ask them to omit details and "flowery language" and distill the information down to its basic nuggets.

Students often find the task of summarizing confusing; initially, they struggle to identify what material to keep and what to omit. The three recommendations for classroom practice emphasize the importance of helping students deal with this confusion by providing structures that guide them through the process of summarizing:

- Teach students the rule-based summarizing strategy.
- Use summary frames.
- Engage students in reciprocal teaching.

### Teach students the rule-based summarizing strategy

It is often helpful to have a well-defined set of steps or rules to follow when learning a process. The rule-based summarizing strategy helps to demystify the process of summarizing by providing explicit, concrete steps to follow. It provides guidance that helps students decide what information to keep and what to omit when summarizing information. The rules are as follows:

1. Take out material that is not important to understanding.
2. Take out words that repeat information.
3. Replace a list of things with one word that describes them (e.g., replace "oak, elm, and maple" with "trees").
4. Find a topic sentence or create one if it is missing.

Some teachers extend this set of rules and ask students to share their summary drafts with other students and then make revisions. To help students learn how to apply the rule-based strategy, teachers should model the process in a fairly detailed manner, as illustrated in the example that follows.

## Example

Ms. Peschel is walking her 9th grade students through the rule-based summarizing strategy in the context of a science unit about weather. She knows it is important for her students to have a working knowledge of the content they are being asked to summarize, so she waits until the middle of the unit to introduce the process of summarizing. She thus ensures that students will be able to focus on the process, using information with which they are familiar, rather than struggle to learn a new process and new content at the same time. She begins by presenting her students with a short text on tornadoes (see Figure 6.1).

---

FIGURE 6.1
### Summarizing Strategy Sample Passage

**Tornadoes and Other Twisting Windstorms**

There are many types of twisting windstorms that form over land and water. One type, a tornado, forms over land and is incredibly powerful. It begins high in a massive convective storm comprised of cumulonimbus clouds. Those who have experienced a tornado's fierce winds and explosive sounds explain that the noises remind them of a freight train and that the experience is extremely frightening. Tornadoes, or twisters, can occur any time of year, but they are most prevalent in April, May, June, July, and August. Cyclones and dust devils are other types of twisting windstorms, but these windstorms are different from tornadoes in several important ways.

Cyclones form over water and, depending on their strength and location, can be referred to as hurricanes, typhoons, or tropical storms. Cyclones rotate counterclockwise in the northern hemisphere and clockwise in the southern hemisphere. Hurricanes, a well-known example of cyclones, develop over the warm waters of the Atlantic Ocean in the northern hemisphere. As they build in strength and move onto land, they bring powerful winds, heavy rain, and damaging surf, and they can generate tornadoes. Unlike tornadoes, which last only a short time and cover a small area, hurricanes cover large areas and often last for days.

Dust devils are much weaker than tornadoes and hurricanes and are not associated with storms. The winds in dust devils are slow, compared to those in hurricanes and tornadoes. Dust devil wind speeds are between 4 and 35 miles per hour. Winds in tornadoes and hurricanes can be greater than 100 miles per hour. Unlike their larger relatives, dust devils are small in size and have a short duration—just a few minutes.

She first asks her students to read the passage silently to themselves. Ms. Peschel then explains that she is going to use a think-aloud approach to demonstrate the rule-based strategy for summarizing. She talks her students through the process as follows: "I'm going to think aloud as I apply the rules of this strategy. As you follow along, see if my thinking makes sense to you and write down any questions you have, as well as parts of the process that are clear and useful. We will discuss your questions and what you have learned at the end of my demonstration.

"Summarizing is different from retelling, where we keep lots of detailed information. The rules for summarizing indicate that we should take out information that is not important to understanding, take out words that repeat information, and substitute one term for a list of terms. Look at this text on tornadoes. The first paragraph contains background information, some of which is trivial. There are a few words that can be omitted, and I can combine some of the ideas and substitute words. I also see something redundant: *a massive convective storm* and *cumulonimbus clouds* are similar, so I'll delete one of them. Come to think of it, the list of months is not very important, so I will group them together using a phrase. Here's my first paragraph now."

Ms. Peschel then writes her newly summarized paragraph on the board:

*Twisting windstorms form over land and water. Tornadoes form in massive convective storm clouds. People say tornadoes sound like freight trains and are frightening. Tornadoes occur most often in warm months. Cyclones and dust devils are also twisting storms, but they are different in many ways.*

Ms. Peschel continues with her think-aloud as she summarizes the other paragraphs, taking out trivial and redundant parts and, when necessary, grouping information. When she is finished, Ms. Peschel says to her class, "Finally, I can put it all together. Do the new paragraphs make sense? I was able to take out a lot without losing clarity. What do you think of my final summary?"

After this detailed description of her own thinking, Ms. Peschel asks her students to work with partners and try out the rule-based summarizing strategy with a different textbook passage.

When all of the teachers in a school agree to use the rule-based summarizing strategy on a consistent basis, it enhances the overall learning environment for students. Students do not have to alter their thinking about how to summarize as they move from classroom to classroom or grade level to grade level. For example, if a 7th grade class has been taught to use the rule-based summarizing strategy, students feel more confident and less confused at the beginning of 8th grade when the teacher asks them to summarize a poem about summer. Teachers know that students are already familiar with the rule-based summarizing strategy, and they are able to use the relevant academic language to prompt a familiar task for students.

## Use summary frames

Research indicates that being aware of the explicit structure of information helps to summarize and remember that information (Broer et al., 2002; Meyer, Middlemiss, Theodorou, Brezinski, & McDougall, 2002; Meyer & Poon, 2001). Using summary frames is one way that teachers can help students understand and use the structure of different kinds of text to summarize information. A summary frame is a series of questions designed to highlight the critical elements of a specific text pattern. Students use their responses to those questions to create a summary of the key information.

We present six basic frames into which text can be placed: narrative, topic-restriction-illustration, definition, argumentation, problem–solution, and conversation. Each of these frames has a number of questions associated with it that help students identify the kind of text they are reading and key points from that reading. To encourage use of the frames, teachers can create posters for each type and hang them in the classroom, provide a reference handout for students to use when necessary, or post a definition of each type to a classroom wiki or website.

We include each frame below with the corresponding set of questions and an example that illustrates how teachers might use the frame to help students summarize a particular type of text.

**Narrative Frame**

1. Who are the main characters? What distinguishes them from the other characters?
2. When and where did the story take place? What were the circumstances?
3. What prompted the action in the story?
4. How did the characters express their feelings?
5. What did the main characters decide to do? Did they set a goal? What was it?
6. How did the main characters try to accomplish their goals?
7. What were the consequences?

A 5th grade class is reading the first chapter of C. S. Lewis's *The Lion, the Witch, and the Wardrobe*. The teacher asks her students to summarize what they have read so far. At first, her students seem confused about what material is important to understanding. Once prompted with questions from the narrative frame, however, her students are able to identify key points of the chapter, such as what distinguishes Lucy from her other siblings and which event started the children's adventures in Narnia. She then has her students write a quick blog post that summarizes the chapter.

**Topic-Restriction-Illustration Frame**

1. What is the general statement or *topic*?
2. What information narrows or *restricts* the general statement or topic?
3. What examples *illustrate* the topic or restriction?

Mrs. Johansen wants to provide her students with a review of animal classification, which they learned the previous year. She decides to use her school's subscription to BrainPOP to engage her students in summarizing what they know about mammals, birds, reptiles, amphibians, and fish. She organizes her students into five groups and has each group watch a movie about a particular class of animals. She encourages each group to pause the movie at key points and use a topic-restriction-illustration frame to help them summarize the movie. One group's work appears as so:

| | |
|---|---|
| Topic: | *Fish* |
| Restriction: | *Fish have a backbone and are cold-blooded or ectothermic. Most fish have gills, scales, and fins.* |
| Illustration: | *Fish are divided into three classes: bony (goldfish), cartilaginous (sharks), and agnathan (lampreys).* |
| Summary: | *Fish are cold-blooded animals with backbones. There are three types of fish, which are based on skeletal composition.* |

### Definition Frame

1. What is being defined?
2. To which general category does the item belong?
3. What characteristics separate the item from the other things in the general category?
4. What are some different types or classes of the item being defined?

Students in Ms. Lewers's 10th grade class use a variety of Web 2.0 tools throughout the year to help them write, collaborate, and share resources. Knowing that these tools will be new to some of her students, she engages her students in a web scavenger hunt to learn the following terms: *wiki, blog, social bookmarking, Web 2.0,* and *image/video hosting*. Students pair up and use a definition frame to help them capture key ideas about each term. Below is an example using a definition frame.

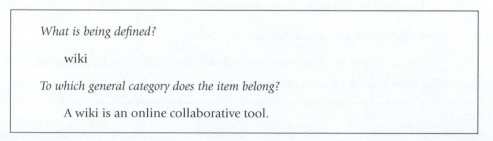

*What is being defined?*

wiki

*To which general category does the item belong?*

A wiki is an online collaborative tool.

*continued*

*What characteristics separate the item from other things in the general category?*

A wiki helps people create and edit websites without having to know special code or have special software. Typically, any member of a wiki community can edit the page but not at the same time as someone else.

*What are some different types or classes of the item being defined?*

PBWorks, Wikispaces, Google Sites

*Summary*

A wiki is a collaborative tool that helps people create and edit websites together. Some examples include PBWorks, Wikispaces, and Google Sites. Usually, only one person can edit a wiki page at a time.

## Argumentation Frame

1. What is the basic claim or focus of the information?
2. What information is presented that leads to a claim?
3. What examples or explanations support the claim?
4. What restricts the claim? What evidence counters the claim?

Mrs. Vogel uses the argumentation frame to help her 9th grade social studies students summarize a short television news story about multistate lotteries. She first presents the argumentation questions and then asks students to answer them in writing as they view the news story. One student, Maurie, answers the argumentation frame questions in the following way:

*What is the basic claim or focus of the information?*

Our state should join a multistate lottery.

*What information is presented that leads to a claim?*

The state benefits from state lottery games, and multistate lottery games offer more money for state programs.

*What examples or explanations support the claim?*

Multistate lotteries will give the state a source of revenue to spend on health care and safety problems in public schools. People drive out of state to purchase tickets for big, multistate lottery games, but that money should stay in our state. Multistate lotteries are the only way for people in smaller states to win really big jackpots. Tickets for the big lottery games are usually cheap, but they give players the potential to win millions of dollars.

*What restricts the claim?*

Our state already has lottery games.

*Summary*

Although our state already has lottery games, joining a multistate lottery would provide more benefits to the state. Joining a multistate lottery would keep more money in the state and allow players to win bigger jackpots.

## Problem–Solution Frame

1. What is the problem?
2. What is a possible solution?
3. What is another possible solution?
4. Which solution has the best chance of succeeding and why?

Middle school students are asked to research a recent oil spill in the Gulf of Mexico. They read several articles and listen to podcasts from scientists, geologists, conservationists, and politicians about what should be done to minimize the spill's impact on the environment. The stated problem is that crude oil and tar will have a detrimental effect on marine life, the coastline, and land animals that depend on marine life for sustenance. Several solutions are proposed that revolve around the idea of containing the oil, such as using containment booms or building barrier islands. Other solutions attempt to disperse the oil with chemicals. Finally, a third category of solutions focuses on the idea of removing the oil by burning, filtering, or collecting it. Each of these solutions poses its own set of drawbacks, which the students include in their write-ups and presentations. To summarize the various points of view, they use the problem–solution frame for each possible solution.

**Conversation Frame**

1. How did the members of the conversation greet one another?
2. What question or topic was insinuated, revealed, or referred to?
3. How did the conversation progress?
4. How did the conversation conclude?

For a study on U.S. politics, a high school civics teacher asks his students to use a conversation frame as they watch the same political figure be interviewed by two different television hosts with decidedly different political views. As the students use the conversation frame, they notice that the greetings are very similar, with polite head nods and handshakes, as are the topics addressed by the interview questions, which usually refer to a recent initiative or speech given by the politician. Students also notice a distinct difference when the political figure is interviewed by someone from her own party versus the opposing party. The opposing party interview tends to include more interruptions and references to previous statements the politician had made. In the same-party interview, the politician is interrupted less and asked more questions about how her ideas are an improvement over the status quo. This interview also ends on a more upbeat note than the opposing party interview. Using the conversation frame helps students gain a powerful insight on how speeches and interviews can be slanted in favor of or against a person.

## Engage students in reciprocal teaching

A common strategy for teaching students how to summarize is reciprocal teaching, which is used primarily with expository text (Palincsar & Brown, 1985). When students first learn how to use reciprocal teaching, the teacher models how to use the four comprehension strategies that constitute reciprocal teaching: summarizing, questioning, clarifying, and predicting. Gradually, the teacher releases implementation of the four strategies to student control. During reciprocal teaching, students assume four roles (summarizer, questioner, clarifier, and predictor) and take turns leading the discussion. One student can play all four roles, or different students can assume each role.

The summarizer reads a short passage and summarizes what has been read, heard, or seen. Other students may add to the summary at this time. When students first begin reciprocal teaching, they are generally focused at the sentence and paragraph levels. As they become more proficient with the technique, they are able to integrate information from the multiple paragraph and passage levels.

After the summarizer finishes, the questioner asks questions that are designed to help identify important information. He or she presents information in question form, and the rest of the group answers the questions in order to go deeper into the text. As students learn this process, they are taught to generate questions at deeper levels. For example, teachers might require students to ask questions that require the group to infer or apply new information from a text.

The clarifier, as the name suggests, clarifies any vocabulary words, pronunciations, or terms the group may not already know or understand well. This student is taught to look for aspects of a passage that might make it hard for his or her classmates to comprehend the passage and do what is necessary to make the meaning clear (e.g., reread, ask for help).

The final role in this process is that of the predictor. Before the group moves forward to the next passage, this student asks for predictions about what will happen next. He or she can record the predictions on chart paper or a computer and return to these predictions for verification after reading. To do this successfully, the predictor must review the relevant information that the group already possesses about the topic. By generating these predictions, students have a purpose for continued reading—to confirm their predictions.

## Example

Ms. Renier's 10th grade family and consumer sciences class is reading a magazine article about the rise of childhood obesity. For this activity, she organizes students in groups of four and assigns each student one of the roles of reciprocal teaching: summarizer, questioner, clarifier, and predictor. She first asks students to form "expert groups" according to their roles (all summarizers meet in a group, for example). Together, students read the article through the lens of their particular roles. Each role has been assigned a set of sentence starters that will help students find and articulate the appropriate information (Hill & Björk, 2008). Once they reconvene with their original groups, students take turns fulfilling the requirements of their respective roles. This process helps students capture key points, work together as a team, and gain a collective understanding of the topic.

During this activity, Jacinta initially struggles with her role as questioner, since some of the vocabulary in the article is unfamiliar to her. However, after she receives a list of question starters from her teacher and works with her peers who have similar roles, she is able to learn the vocabulary and help her team formulate effective questions. Rehearsing her learning with a smaller group of peers gives her more confidence than she would normally feel in large group settings.

## Classroom Practice for Note Taking

Note taking does not mean simply copying everything that you read or hear. Verbatim notes are not effective. Trying to capture everything does not allow you to process the knowledge or assimilate it into your own understanding. Effective note taking requires students to determine what is most important and then state that information in a condensed form.

Students often struggle with this strategy because note-taking strategies are not intuitive. The recommendations for classroom practice that we present in this chapter reflect research evidence that supports the idea that students need explicit instruction in note taking and that guided note taking is more effective than unstructured note taking:

- Give students teacher-prepared notes.
- Teach students a variety of note-taking formats.
- Provide opportunities for students to revise their notes and use them for review.

### Give students teacher-prepared notes

Ask a group of adults if they can recall actually being taught how to take notes. Then ask those individuals who answered in the affirmative how old they were when this happened. In all likelihood, relatively few people will be able to say *yes* to the first question. Of those who can, most report that they learned how to take notes in middle school or early high school, and the most common format they mention is formal outlining. Although an argument could be made that formal outlines have their place in organizing information, very few of us actually use this format when we try to quickly capture information during a lecture or presentation.

One teacher recalls the first time someone actually taught her how to take notes.

"No one taught me a useful note-taking method until my high school biology class. The teacher would set up her overhead projector (this was in the 80s) and start lecturing. Every time she hit upon a key point or list, however, she'd stop and write down what our notes should say. She didn't use capital letters and Roman numerals but rather a series of bullet points, arrows, and stars. She would encourage us to draw little pictures out to the side; for example, draw a sun, a tree, and various arrows to remember the process for plant respiration. Finally, she would say, 'Now I don't want these notes to look like they currently do when you're finished with them. I want to see them highlighted, underlined. I want to know that you used them for studying.' To this day, this is how I take notes. I'm often using an informal bulleted outline on my computer and adding links instead of pictures, but it's basically the same process."

The biology teacher demonstrates one way to provide teacher-prepared notes: create notes for students as information is presented. By providing her class with an example, the teacher models how to create well-organized notes. She addresses a problem that interferes with students' ability to take good notes: students may not intuitively realize there should be a pattern in their notes that shows main ideas and supporting details.

Teacher-prepared notes can also be in the form of a template that the teacher prepares and distributes to students. By using this approach, the teacher models how to take notes and provides a structure that demonstrates which topic areas are most important. In addition, the notes themselves can be differentiated so students who have less background knowledge related to the topic or who have less well-developed organizational skills receive more complete notes than other students. This allows each student to access the same information but through a slightly different avenue.

## Example

Marty, a 1st grader, is learning about place value and the base ten system. His teacher has created teacher-prepared notes to help Marty organize the information he is learning. She has also provided a picture of a unit, ten, and hundred, but she left room for Marty to write the numbers, what each place value is a set of, and what the pictures remind him of. (Figure 6.2 shows Marty's finished notes.) Marty is easily able to picture the difference between the three place values with the pictures. He is also able to concentrate on writing key words and information, since his teacher has already provided sentence stems and labels.

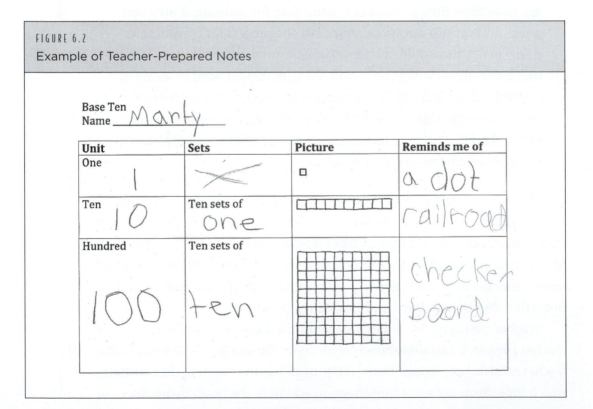

FIGURE 6.2
Example of Teacher-Prepared Notes

Base Ten
Name __Marty__

| Unit | Sets | Picture | Reminds me of |
|---|---|---|---|
| One  1 | | □ | a dot |
| Ten  10 | Ten sets of one | | railroad |
| Hundred  100 | Ten sets of ten | | checker board |

## Teach students a variety of note-taking formats

Research indicates that it is important to provide students with a variety of modes for note taking (Piolat, Olive, & Kellogg, 2005). By having students write words and draw pictures of what they are learning, teachers help them use a variety of strategies to understand and remember new information. This recommendation makes intuitive sense; it is likely that different students prefer different formats for note taking. When students know a variety of formats, they can choose the format that works best for them for a particular project. Three formats that have been found to be useful are webbing, informal outlining, and combination notes.

Webbing is nonlinear and uses shapes, colors, and arrows to show relationships between and among ideas. Allowing time for students to share with other students the thinking behind their webs provides opportunities for them to rehearse their learning, use relevant vocabulary, and deepen their understanding. As students share their thinking, they learn from their peers and may see a need to return to their webs and make corrections or additions (Robinson et al., 1998; Stone & Urquhart, 2008).

Figure 6.3 is a web (created by high school biology students) that shows how some of the "big ideas" from nanotechnology correlate to the classroom instruction about cell structure and function. For this web, the students used an online software tool called Webspiration.

Although some students like the web view, others prefer an outline view. Some may write their notes by hand, whereas other students type their outlines on the computer. For example, one student simply creates information outlines using the bullet feature in her word processing software. Another student uses a traditional spiral-bound notebook to put main ideas in a center circle with supporting details surrounding the main idea. He then writes his notes in paragraph form. A third student uses an iPad app that allows him to handwrite notes, draw webs, and record audio to help him remember.

A third type of note taking, combination notes, includes both linguistic and nonlinguistic representations. In this format, students write key ideas down the left side of a piece of paper or a screen and then draw or paste corresponding pictures down the right side. At the bottom, students capture two

FIGURE 6.3

Web Format for Note Taking

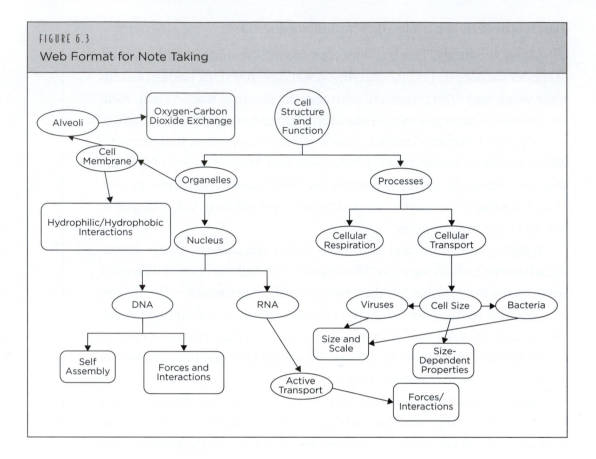

to five key ideas from what they read. The example that follows illustrates the use of combination notes.

## Example

Ms. Simpson is working with her 4th grade social studies students on the rights and responsibilities of citizenship in order to meet the curriculum benchmark: "Know that a citizen is a legally recognized member of the United States who has certain rights and privileges and certain responsibilities (e.g., privileges such as the right to vote and hold public office and responsibilities such as respecting the law, voting, paying taxes, serving on juries)." She provides her students with an advance organizer as a form of teacher-prepared notes. On it, she includes the terms *rights, responsibilities, common good, citizen,* and *law.* She decides to show a video titled "Rights and Responsibilities" and use the advance organizer to take notes. Her plan is to have students use the combination notes process to gain a deeper understanding of the topic.

Jessica, Alyssa, and Valerie are working together. As they watch the video, each one of them takes notes on the advance organizer. After the video ends, Ms. Simpson tells her students to compare their notes with those taken by the other group members and write one complete sentence for each of the five terms on the advance organizer. Jessica, Alyssa, and Valerie work together to come up with their five sentences. They incorporate ideas from each of their individual notes but realize they have much better points by working together.

After giving the class time to develop the five main points, Ms. Simpson distributes a blank template and tells each group to write those points on the left side of the page and then draw a picture that represents each point on the right side. Jessica, Alyssa, and Valerie divide their labors on this activity and each one begins drawing. After they finish their pictures, they explain to one another why they drew what they did.

For the final phase of the process, Ms. Simpson tells students to review their notes and, at the bottom of the page, write a two or three sentence summary of the five main points. Though Jessica, Alyssa, and Valerie had to work hard to summarize their five points, they realize they have a good handle on citizens' rights and responsibilities by the end of the activity, and they are all proud of their work (see Figure 6.4).

It is important to note that in addition to having preferences for different formats, students may differ in the amount of notes they need to take, and that amount might vary from learning unit to learning unit depending on the topic. This reflects students' different levels of background knowledge. As teachers help students develop their note-taking skills, they should keep this in mind so that their feedback guides students to consider how many notes are enough for them. In other words, teachers should not advise students to keep their notes short or to capture as much as possible. Students should take the amount of notes that will serve them well when they use those notes for learning and review. Providing opportunities for students to reflect on their level of knowledge about a topic before and after a learning unit compared to the amount of notes they took will help them gauge how many and what kind of notes are enough.

## Provide opportunities for students to revise their notes and use them for review

You can help students understand that note taking is a purposeful activity by systematically providing opportunities for them to add to and revise their notes as their understanding of a topic increases (Anderson & Armbruster, 1986; Kobayashi, 2006; Makany et al., 2009). To encourage revision of notes, ask students to leave a space between each note they take. By doing this, they will create space to add to their notes over time (Anderson & Armbruster, 1986; Denner, 1986; Einstein, Morris, & Smith, 1985). As students learn more, they are able to elaborate on that learning and improve the quality of their notes.

FIGURE 6.4

**Combination Notes Format for Note Taking**

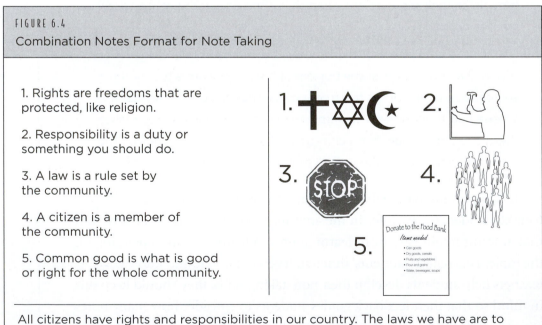

1. Rights are freedoms that are protected, like religion.

2. Responsibility is a duty or something you should do.

3. A law is a rule set by the community.

4. A citizen is a member of the community.

5. Common good is what is good or right for the whole community.

All citizens have rights and responsibilities in our country. The laws we have are to protect the common good and make life better for everyone.

Teachers can use the review and revision process as an opportunity to enhance student learning. For example, as students review their notes, teachers can help them identify and correct misconceptions in notes they previously took. They can also provide corrective feedback on students' note taking that helps students elaborate on their understanding and improve their note-taking skills (Hattie, 1992). The practice of providing time for students to review and revise their notes underscores the point that notes are a work in progress and a valuable tool for learning.

A good reason to revise notes on a regular basis is that the process improves their utility as a study aid; well-designed notes provide a powerful form of review (Kiewra, 1987; Kobayashi, 2006). Students are often unaware of how useful notes can be for review or how to use notes effectively for review. Teachers can help students reap the benefits of well-designed notes by explicitly teaching how to use notes to prepare for tests. This includes explicit instruction about how to structure one's time to use notes adequately. As the example that follows illustrates, even young students can be encouraged to review their notes and use them for learning.

## Example

Mr. Kalmon, a kindergarten teacher, decides to introduce the concept of metamorphosis by reading Eric Carle's *The Very Hungry Caterpillar* to his class. At the end of the story, Mr. Kalmon verbally goes through the questions from the narrative summary frame to make sure all of his students understand the storyline and the concepts that were introduced.

Later that week, Mr. Kalmon rereads the story to his students. Before he begins, he hands out a roll of adding machine paper and a set of crayons to each student. He instructs his students: "I'm going to reread *The Very Hungry Caterpillar,* but this time, I want you to pay close attention to the changes that the caterpillar is going through. Each time it changes, I'm going to stop and ask you to draw a small picture of what you think the caterpillar looks like at that stage."

The narrow width of the paper helps students get the idea that they aren't expected to create a large work of art; rather, they should only capture key ideas from the book. The following week, Mr. Kalmon asks his students to use their drawings and retell the story to a friend. He encourages them to add to their drawings after telling the story themselves and listening to their friends tell the story. In this way, five- and six-year-olds learn how to review and revise their notes and use them to aid in their understanding of academic concepts.

## Summarizing and Note Taking with Today's Learners

In today's world, there is an abundance of rapidly evolving information, and students will benefit throughout their lives from knowing how to summarize information and take notes. Whether they are in a college class, take on-the-job training, or simply watch a how-to video for a home-repair project, today's learners will be well prepared to distill vast amounts of information into manageable chunks of knowledge when they know how to use tools that allow them to save, sort, and capture key points or ideas they want to explore in detail later.

What might it look like for today's learners to use technology for summarizing and note taking in a real-world situation they might encounter as an adult? Imagine that a group of high school students are attending a youth leadership conference. They might use their smartphones to take pictures of book covers or other information in order to remember and access them later. They might save schedules to their laptops or iPads and use tools such as Diigo, Twitter, and Evernote to capture key ideas they are learning. They might download presentation handouts from the conference website and use technology to summarize and take notes about what they hear and see. Best of all, they might share their notes and summaries in real time in a variety of formats, learning from others and contributing to others' learning—even those who are not physically able to attend the conference. For many, learning at this conference would be an organic, user-created, richly shared experience.

Technological tools have the power to help students sift through exponentially expanding information. To use these tools effectively, students need time to dabble with a variety of tools to see which ones best meet their needs for various projects. Schools and districts should focus on teaching students how to use such tools collaboratively and productively to share ideas and learn from others' summarizing and note-taking efforts.

## Tips for Teaching Using Summarizing and Note Taking

1. Post the appropriate steps for rule-based summarizing, and reference the poster as students summarize information.
2. Come to an agreement with colleagues about the version of rule-based summarizing that will be used throughout your school. This makes it possible for students to hear and use the same information in each of their classes and across grade levels.
3. Provide students with opportunities to practice summarizing and note-taking techniques using familiar information before they are expected to use them with new material.
4. Model the note-taking process several times before students are expected to demonstrate an understanding and appropriate use of the various formats.
5. When students practice note taking, provide explicit corrective feedback that helps them elaborate on their understanding and improve their note-taking skills.
6. Instruct students to leave space between each note they take to create room to add to their notes as they continue learning about the topic.
7. Intentionally build time into your lesson plans for students to review and edit their notes. Do not expect students to take care of this important step on their own, especially if they have had no prior experience doing so.
8. When using webbing as a note-taking tool, provide time for students to share their thinking with other students. This provides opportunities for students to rehearse their learning, use relevant vocabulary, and deepen their understanding. In addition, students learn from their peers and may see a need to return to their webs and make corrections or additions.

# 7

# Assigning Homework and Providing Practice

"Attitudes toward homework have historically reflected societal trends and the prevailing educational philosophy of the time, and each swing of the pendulum is colored by unique historical events and sentiments that drove the movement for and against homework."

—Cathy Vatterott, *Rethinking Homework*

Think back to your days as a student. How did you feel about having to do homework? How do your students feel about it now? Do most of your students (or students in your school) complete homework, or do they make excuses, such as the student who claims the dog ate his homework? Do you have evidence that students in your school benefit from doing homework? In the last few years, there have been mixed research reviews on the effectiveness and importance of homework (Kohn, 2006; Marzano & Pickering, 2007), yet most teachers continue to assign homework and believe there is a good reason to do so. In this chapter, we provide information that will help you think carefully about the purpose and effects of assigning homework. We also focus on the importance of providing practice, which we define as opportunities to enhance one's ability to develop proficiency with new skills and processes. We group Assigning Homework and Providing Practice in the same category because both strategies provide students with multiple opportunities to learn a skill or process or to review and apply knowledge.

## Why This Category Is Important

We use "homework" to refer to opportunities for students to learn or review content and skills outside of the regular school day. Homework can also be used as an opportunity to connect background knowledge to an upcoming unit by providing advance organizers such as engaging students in making observations, watching videos, initiating conversations, and completing reading assignments.

"Practice" is the act of repeating a specific skill or reviewing small amounts of information to increase recall, speed, and accuracy. This strategy refers to the need for students to devote time to reviewing what they have learned so that it becomes immediately accessible for cognitive use. This information can be stored in a student's working memory or long-term memory, depending on how often the information is used.

For the 2010 study, McREL researchers calculated an average effect size of 0.13 for Assigning Homework and 0.42 for Providing Practice. The first edition of *Classroom Instruction That Works* reported a combined average effect size of 0.77 for this category. There were few studies that met McREL's criteria for inclusion in the 2010 study, which means that the effect sizes for Assigning Homework and Providing Practice should be interpreted with caution. Our comments about homework reflect the quantitative and descriptive studies included in the 2010 study. Together, these studies suggest a small but positive relationship between the portion of homework that students complete and their achievement levels.

The effects of homework on student achievement are not entirely clear; a number of factors, such as degree of parental involvement and support, homework quality, students' learning preferences, and structure and monitoring of assignments can affect the influence of homework on achievement (Hong, Milgram, & Rowell, 2004; Minotti, 2005). This is one possible reason why there is mixed evidence that shows homework increases student achievement. Nonetheless, many teachers, parents, and students believe that it does (Cooper, 1989; Cooper, Robinson, & Patall, 2006; Gill & Schlossman, 2003). Cooper and colleagues' (2006) meta-analysis of research on homework practice provides support for the positive effects of homework. Using narrative and quantitative techniques, the analysis integrated the results of research on homework from 1987 through 2003 and revealed a positive relationship between homework and achievement with an effect size of 0.60. Other researchers have found no positive relationship between homework and achievement (e.g., Vatterott, 2009).

There is evidence that suggests homework is more effective for older students (middle and high school) than for elementary students (Cooper, Lindsay, Nye, & Greathouse, 1998). Some researchers highlight the negative consequences of homework, including a disruption of family time, physical and emotional fatigue, a lack of access to community and leisure activities, and conflicts between students and their parents (e.g., Coutts, 2004; Warton, 2001). Teachers must carefully weigh both the positive and negative consequences of assigning homework and ensure that their assignments make the best use of students' out-of-school time.

We may hold to the maxim that "practice makes perfect," but research indicates the relationship between practice and academic achievement is somewhat mixed. It seems that not all practice yields improved performance. For example, if students practice a skill incorrectly, they will ultimately have difficulty learning the correct way to perform that skill. "Traditional" homework practice that involves reviewing notes or rereading texts has little effect on achievement; however, it is better than no practice at all (McDaniel, Roediger, & McDermott, 2007). To be effective, practice should be overt, which means it actively involves students recalling material through quizzes, rehearsal, or self-assessment (e.g., flash cards or labeling). When these forms of practice testing occur frequently (at least two or three times during the period between acquisition or presentation of material and final assessment of knowledge), there are greater effects on student achievement than when practice testing occurs less frequently (Karpicke & Roediger, 2008). Testing students at regular intervals throughout a learning period has a positive impact on learning (Carpenter, Pashler, & Cepeda, 2009; Rohrer, Taylor, & Sholar, 2010).

Practice also is more likely to be effective when it requires students to practice more than one skill at a time (Hall, Domingues, & Cavazos, 1994; Rohrer & Taylor, 2007). For example, if students practice finding the radius of a circle given the circumference but not finding the circumference given the radius, or finding measurements of other shapes, those students tend to do less well on tests.

Practice is also more likely to be effective when students can access and use corrective feedback about their performance to determine what and how to practice. When students use this feedback to shape their practice sessions, they improve retention and achievement of the skill or knowledge (Pashler, Rohrer, Cepeda, & Carpenter, 2007). Practice also appears to be more effective when distributed over time rather than massed into a single session (Cepeda, Pashler, Vul, Wixted, & Rohrer, 2006; Donovan & Radosevich, 1999).

## Classroom Practice for Assigning Homework

Given the mixed research results for the effects of homework on student achievement, we encourage teachers to think carefully about their design and use of homework assignments, particularly in elementary school. The recommendations that follow can increase the likelihood that homework yields positive results, but teachers can further enhance their use of homework by monitoring the effects of homework on their students and modifying their practice accordingly.

There are three recommendations for assigning homework to improve student achievement:

- Develop and communicate a district or school homework policy.
- Design homework assignments that support academic learning and communicate their purpose.
- Provide feedback on assigned homework.

### Develop and communicate a district or school homework policy

An established homework policy communicates and clarifies the purpose of homework in your district or school. Establishing a clear set of guidelines that is based on the age of the learner, the expectations for completion, and the relationship between homework and grades provides a manageable framework for collaboration between home and school. It also provides an avenue for student success. A school or, better yet, a district that uses the resource base of parents, teachers, administrators, and students to create, implement, and monitor a homework policy will find that many of the ongoing struggles associated with homework dissipate.

A word of caution about homework policies: they should not restrict a teacher's ability to make judgments about when it is appropriate to assign homework. In other words, policies that state homework *must* be given at particular times (e.g., every night, three times per week) ignore the importance of being intentional about assigning homework. Homework in elementary school should be assigned sparingly. Homework in middle and high school should be assigned as needed, and it should be directly tied to the skills needed for achieving mastery of learning objectives. The following sections include information that can help schools and districts develop effective homework policies.

### Time on homework

Time spent on homework matters; there is a relationship between time spent on homework and academic achievement at all levels (Cooper et al., 2006), but the relationship is stronger for secondary students than for primary and intermediate students. The relationship is not simple, however. A study by Wagner, Schober, and Spiel (2008) found that lower-performing students spent more time on homework than higher-performing students did. In addition, some of the literature on homework suggests that the amount of time spent on homework may be less important than the perceived quality of homework assignments and the level of student effort on those assignments.

Teachers might wonder how much homework is the "right" amount, but the amount of homework that is appropriate varies by grade level. The first edition of this text offered a general rule of 10 minutes times the grade level, and that equation has been endorsed by the National Education Association and the Parent Teacher Association (Vatterott, 2009). Teachers should keep in mind that there is a limit to how much homework students can do and still reap benefits; there are few additional benefits and several possible negative consequences of assignments beyond 90 minutes for middle school students and two hours for high school students (Cooper, 2007). The findings from research on the academic benefits of homework for young children are mixed, and there is disagreement about whether homework should be assigned at all to students in 2nd grade and younger (Vatterott, 2009). Teachers of young children should think carefully about the characteristics of their own students before assigning homework. If they do assign homework, it should be only small amounts, and the effects of the homework on students and their families should be carefully monitored.

**Parent involvement in homework**

Homework often causes friction between parents and teachers, in part because both teachers and parents lack clarity about parental roles and responsibilities related to homework. Although McREL's 1998 meta-analysis suggested that parent involvement should be kept to a minimum, the 2010 analysis suggests that it isn't so much *whether* parents are involved as *how* they are involved. The 2010 study found that homework assignments that involve parent–child interaction may help to improve performance. For example, parents might have discussions with their children about the topics they are studying. In addition to motivating students, such discussions help parents understand the learning objectives and foster communication with teachers about the objectives and their children's progress toward achieving them.

Parents serve an important role in encouraging their children to put forth effort and intellect while completing homework tasks. It should not be necessary or expected that parents act as supplementary teachers or tutors; students should not be assigned homework on skills or processes they are not yet able to perform independently. When students are tasked with homework that involves a skill or process, the purpose of that homework should be to improve speed and accuracy, not to learn the steps or conceptual underpinnings of the skill or process. In other words, if a student says he can't complete the homework because no one at home knew how to help him, then it was premature for the teacher to assign that homework to that student. He had not yet learned the skill or process with enough understanding to be able to do it independently.

To help parents better understand how they can support their children's efforts to complete homework, teachers can share information on different structures and monitoring techniques that parents can use to create conditions at home that match a child's learning preferences. Providing such information during parent workshops and encouraging dialogue about school work between parents and their children has demonstrated positive effects on student achievement in reading (Bailey, Silvern, Brabham, & Ross, 2004). Teachers can encourage parents to have a defined time and place for completing homework with few distractions. They also can help both parents and students understand that parents can help by clarifying questions, such as following the directions, but this is not required to *teach* the skill or activity to the student. Parents and teachers should keep in mind that although it is helpful for parents to create appropriate environments for homework, their involvement in the actual content of the homework is often not beneficial (Balli, 1998; Balli, Demo, & Wedman, 1998).

### Design homework assignments that support academic learning and communicate their purpose

Homework should support rather than discourage student learning. It should be assigned to help students prepare for instruction, to review or practice, or to extend learning opportunities. It should never be used as punishment or in place of classroom instruction. Homework should not be considered to be a measure of rigor of the curriculum; the fact that students have homework or a particular amount of homework does not mean that the school has a rigorous curriculum. The purpose of homework should be clearly articulated to students and stakeholders.

A common purpose for homework, and one we emphasize in this chapter, is to provide students with opportunities to practice skills and processes in order to increase their speed, accuracy, fluency, and conceptual understanding. Students should be fairly familiar with the relevant skill if they are going to practice it for homework. If they are not, the practice will be inefficient, and students might learn the skill incorrectly or have their misconceptions reinforced—a clear case of imperfect practice yielding imperfect results! Another general purpose of homework is to prepare students to extend their learning, either by providing opportunities to learn new content or to elaborate on content that has already been introduced. Unlike the case of homework for practicing skills, students do not need an in-depth understanding of the content to complete this type of homework successfully.

## Example

To prepare for and get students interested in an upcoming unit on lunar phases, Ms. Lopez asks her middle school students to observe and sketch the phases of the moon over the course of the following two weeks. Before the unit even begins, her students start to notice that as the moon gets fuller, it also rises later in the day. After the full moon, students notice that the moon appears later and later until they are no longer awake when the moon rises. This experience leads to intriguing discussions about their observations as Ms. Lopez starts the first lesson in the unit.

Within any school or district, teachers' views on the purposes of homework may vary along a spectrum—from homework as a way to extend learning opportunities to homework as punishment when students do not behave in class. Within this spectrum are various other reasons for why homework should be assigned (e.g., to develop students' study habits or critical-thinking skills, to inform parents about what their children are learning). Ideally, districts will involve a group of stakeholders to clearly define the purpose(s) of homework. At a minimum, the purpose of homework should be clearly defined within a school, but if that does not occur, then teachers should be clear with students and parents about their purposes for assigning homework. When teachers in a school have a shared understanding of and commitment to how homework will be used to improve student achievement, students reap the benefits. Taking time to fully define the general purpose of homework is the beginning to a successful, student-oriented learning culture.

## Provide feedback on assigned homework

Providing feedback on homework assignments benefits students, particularly when that feedback is in the form of written comments or grades (Walberg, 1999). To be consistent with the purposes of using homework as an opportunity to improve students' speed and accuracy with skills and processes, to prepare students for new content, or to elaborate on content just introduced, it is better to support homework assignments with feedback in the form of comments rather than grades. House (2004) shows that checking homework during class time (which usually involves determining whether an answer is right or wrong and providing no corrective feedback) appears to be unrelated to, if not negatively correlated with, achievement. If teachers want to give students grades for completing homework (for example, as part of a grade for effort), those grades should be considered as part of students' nonacademic performance.

Following the recommendations for Providing Feedback (see Chapter 1), homework should first be aligned to a learning objective, and the feedback should be tied to that objective. This does not imply that every assignment should be graded; rather, students should receive feedback that indicates next steps for growth toward proficiency. Providing feedback (rather than grades) on homework can encourage students to take risks and show teachers aspects of their conceptual understanding that they might not have revealed on a graded assignment.

There are a variety of ways that feedback can be provided (e.g., teacher–student conferences, class discussions, peer review). If teachers have insufficient time to ensure that students receive feedback on every assignment, they should reconsider how feedback is provided (peer, whole group, written) and the amount of homework assigned. The example that follows demonstrates how one teacher changed her practice related to homework to ensure that it was a valuable addition to her students' learning experiences.

### Example

At the beginning of the school year, Ms. Ling's 7th grade life science students seemed eager to do their science homework, but lately, only a few of the students have been completing homework assignments. Ms. Ling decides that she will hold a class meeting to talk about the importance of practicing new learning both in class and at home. As the meeting begins, students are hesitant to express their feelings about the recently assigned homework. Finally, Zach speaks up and explains that he is struggling with his homework because he doesn't feel he fully understands the work. Therefore, he is lost when he sits down at home to complete his assignments. Sara speaks next and explains that several teachers assign homework on the same nights, which creates an overload of work with little time to complete each of the assignments. Juan says that he already knows the information and sees little reason to complete "busy work." Other students in the class express similar feelings.

Although some of the student comments are not what Ms. Ling expects, she takes the input into consideration as she designs upcoming lessons and the accompanying homework. For Zach and students like him, she provides additional practice time that is accompanied by corrective feedback before assigning homework. Ms. Ling also works with her colleagues to use an online shared calendar to inform one another about test schedules and assigned homework each week.

It is Juan's comment that troubles Ms. Ling the most. She realizes that giving the same homework to all of her students is not a productive way to help students realize their potential, so she begins to differentiate homework assignments, tailoring assignments to provide individuals or small groups of students with the types of experiences they need to achieve the learning objectives. These varied homework assignments are subtle. For example, students who need to review basic concepts can answer review questions in the back of the textbook. Those who need an extra challenge, however, are asked to refer to the class wiki where Ms. Ling gives more in-depth assignments, such as creating a podcast of what they learned or creating a dynamic study guide to help them and their classmates study for an upcoming exam. Her new approach alleviates the problem of missing homework and creates a positive learning environment.

## Classroom Practice for Providing Practice

Practice is important for mastering skills, but, like homework, practice must have certain characteristics to produce the desired results. The following recommendations for practice help teachers make the most of this strategy:

- Clearly identify and communicate the purpose of practice activities.

- Design practice sessions that are short, focused, and distributed over time.
- Provide feedback on practice sessions.

## Clearly identify and communicate the purpose of practice activities

As stated previously, practice must tightly align with learning objectives and provide students with opportunities to deepen their understanding or become faster and more proficient at a skill. Students are much more inclined to stay engaged in practice activities and elaborate on their learning when they fully understand the purpose and expected outcomes of those activities. Students should be engaged in practice with both declarative and procedural knowledge. Without knowing why a certain skill is important or what to do with content, there is a disconnect between the practice and the expected learning outcome. In other words, students should be able to clearly articulate what and why they are practicing. To keep parents informed about the content being studied, the expectations for practice, and the criteria for high-quality work, teachers can communicate through newsletters, blogs, shared calendars, and websites. For example, at the beginning of each month, a teacher might send home a newsletter that includes a description of the units students will study and the learning objectives that are the focus of those units. The newsletter could include sample questions or topics related to the units that parents could discuss with their children.

### Example

Mr. Newbill, a 3rd grade teacher, devotes the first 10 minutes of the math block for his students to work on a multiplication family of their choice. Students may play an online game, use flashcards with a peer, or play one of several board games that help them with their multiplication facts. One student, Claire, asks why she must remember these facts when it is so simple to look them up on a calculator or cell phone. Mr. Newbill responds first by acknowledging Claire for asking such an excellent question. He then seizes this opportunity to talk about why certain facts or skills are recommended for memorization. He gathers his

3rd graders together as a group and shows them an example of much larger problems they will be working on soon: 3,620 × 43.

"I'm going to solve this problem for you as you watch," he says, "and I'm going to think out loud as I do so. I want you to notice how quickly I'm able to solve the problem since I've memorized my facts." When he is finished, he demonstrates solving a similar problem, this time using a calculator to first figure each fact. The students are amused; yet they also now understand the need for not having to look up each fact.

That afternoon, Mr. Newbill describes this experience in his weekly blog, as he wonders if many parents have similar questions as Claire. He explains the experience his class had together that day and why he plans for brief, meaningful practice sessions before each math lesson. Several educators respond to his blog, sharing their experiences and insights about the need for practice and memorizing facts in the digital age.

## Design practice sessions that are short, focused, and distributed over time

It is easier for students to concentrate on mastering a skill or process when practice sessions are short. Short practice sessions encourage students to make efficient use of their practice time. If practice sessions are long, they can lead to fatigue or boredom and decrease students' motivation to learn the relevant skill or process (Rohrer & Taylor, 2007).

Focused practice is designed to target specific aspects of more complex skills and processes. This type of practice is important when students find some aspect of a complex, multistep process or skill—such as the writing process or the scientific method—particularly challenging to master. Focused practice does not mean isolated practice. Rather, teachers provide students with practice sessions that target the difficult aspect(s) of a skill or process but still engage them in the overall skill or process.

Learning new content does not happen quickly; it requires practice sessions that are spread over time. Students need to practice a skill at least 24 times before they reach 80 percent competency (Anderson, 1995; Newell & Rosenbloom, 1981). Frequent, short practice sessions early in the learning process result in the greatest amount of learning, which gradually decreases as students refine their knowledge and skill sets. It takes a great deal of practice for students to perform a skill with speed and accuracy. When they first learn a skill or process, students should have practice sessions that are immediate and close together (massed); over time, practice sessions can be spaced out (distributed). Figure 7.1 illustrates massed and distributed practice. It is important to provide sufficient and guided practice prior to moving students to independent practice. If this is not done, students might practice incorrectly or develop bad habits and errors as they execute the process.

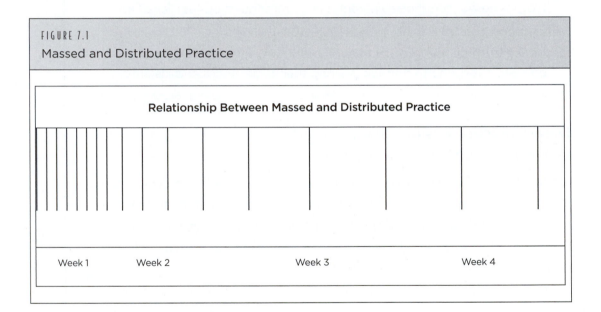

FIGURE 7.1
Massed and Distributed Practice

Relationship Between Massed and Distributed Practice

Week 1    Week 2    Week 3    Week 4

Before students move to independent practice, it is important to check that they understand how the skill or process works. Without this conceptual understanding, students can only use procedures in shallow or ineffective ways. Practice sessions should provide opportunities for students to adapt or shape skills as they learn them. During this phase, students build their conceptual understanding of the skill or process rather than focus on performing the skill with speed. Practice sessions should focus on a deep examination of the skill or process. In mathematics, for example, this might mean working through only a few sample problems that illustrate different aspects of the process rather than solving a whole page of problems. Ensuring students have the opportunities they need to develop conceptual understanding takes careful planning. When planning a unit, identify specific problems or scenarios that you think will help students develop conceptual understanding of the skills and processes that will be introduced during the unit and, for future reference, document those that work best (Clement, Lockhead, & Mink, 1979; Davis, 1984; Mathematical Sciences Education Board, 1990; Romberg & Carpenter, 1986).

The example that follows illustrates how the recommendation for developing conceptual understanding and providing practice might play out in a high school Latin class.

## Example

Magistra Metz, a high school Latin teacher, is preparing her new Latin I students to learn the endings of the first declension of nouns. She begins the unit by going over the concepts of declensions and associated genders. The idea of words having gender is new to many of her students, and they struggle with the idea that an entire category of words can be thought of as feminine or masculine. After much discussion about the content, Magistra Metz knows that her students not only need to understand the first declension but also need a mechanism for memorizing the endings. She reveals a chart of the appropriate endings on her interactive whiteboard (see Downloadable Figure 6).

Magistra Metz then hands out several game boards she has created on which students must place word endings in the correct position. She asks her students to work in pairs to place the endings, allowing them to "race" during the second and third rounds. As her students master the endings, she eventually has them place words from a Latin sentence in the correct place on the chart.

By first ensuring that students understand the concept, and then giving them time to practice the skill in a motivating way, Magistra Metz models best practices on homework and practice. Specifically, she gives students an opportunity to build conceptual understanding before assigning homework that they will find immediately useful the following day.

## Provide feedback on practice sessions

As mentioned previously, skills and processes develop over time. Practice sessions when students are first learning a skill should be considered formative practice sessions—students are developing their understanding of what the process is and shaping their knowledge and use of it. It is critical that students receive specific feedback during formative practice sessions to help them understand which aspect(s) of the skill or process they are not performing appropriately. This information helps teachers and students design subsequent practice sessions to address those areas. Formative practice should not be graded. Simply giving a grade on a practice activity does not provide students with the information they need to shape their practice and improve their performance. After students have had many opportunities for formative practice, teachers can provide summative practice opportunities, which focus on checking speed and accuracy. Only summative practice opportunities should be graded and only after students have had a chance to make changes in their performance in response to feedback. The following example illustrates how a 1st grade teacher designed practice sessions and provided feedback to help her students improve their performance.

### Example

Ms. Trujillo has been working with her 1st graders on reading fluency. Many of them are able to decode words successfully, but they haven't reached a comfortable reading speed that allows them to comprehend the text at a deep level. With her school's recent purchase of 25 iPod Touch devices, she decides to use the voice recorder application not only to model fluent reading for her students but also to make it possible for them to record, listen to, and share their reading for improvement.

To begin, Ms. Trujillo records herself reading a short story and places this recording on each device. She shows the class how to access the recording and follow along in their texts. She then teaches her students how to record their own voices, listen to their recordings, and share their recordings with her via e-mail. (Each device was equipped with its own generic e-mail such as iPod1@WestElementary.co.k12.us.) After students have gotten comfortable with the process, Ms. Trujillo notices several improvements over her previous methods of practicing fluency. She can code the students' fluency at any time on her computer, she no longer has to arrange for individual meetings with each student to test fluency, and she notices that students have started self-correcting themselves. After Ms. Trujillo listens to and codes the recording, she sends students individual voice recordings, commending them on their hard work and giving one or two specific suggestions for future practice.

## Assigning Homework and Providing Practice with Today's Learners

Today's teachers and learners have access to a wide variety of tools that allow many methods of practicing a concept and accessing information outside of regular class time. These tools not only give students "anytime, anyplace" access but also provide them with multiple avenues to learn a concept. When used to introduce information or review for homework, they provide engaging alternatives to worksheets and often have the added feature of giving immediate feedback.

For example, many teachers now use video podcasting (vodcasting) to capture key points in their lectures. Students can either download these to personal devices or simply watch and listen to them online. Technology also provides entertaining games that help students study key concepts and skills. The plethora of educational apps available for handheld devices attests to the popularity of using games to revisit content and practice basic skills. At the time of writing this book, there were more than 10,000 educational apps available for various devices.

## Tips for Teaching Using Homework and Practice

1. Always ask, "What learning will result from this homework assignment?" The goal of your instruction should be to design homework that results in meaningful learning.

2. Assign homework to help students deepen their understanding of content, practice skills in order to become faster or more proficient, or learn new content on a surface level.

3. Check that students are able to perform required skills and tasks independently before asking them to complete homework assignments.

4. Consider parents and guardians to be your allies when it comes to homework. Understand their constraints, and, when home circumstances present challenges, consider alternative approaches to support students as they complete homework assignments (e.g., before- or after-school programs, additional parent outreach).

5. When planning a unit, think carefully about how you will space practice sessions. Practice sessions need to be close together when students first learn a skill or process but more spread out later in the learning process to ensure students learn the skill to the proficient level.

6. Ask students to record practice sessions outside of class, particularly for music or performing arts classes. Teachers can provide feedback to students or ask students to provide their own feedback on these sessions.

# Part III

## Helping Students Extend and Apply Knowledge

# 8

# Identifying Similarities and Differences

"Learning processes often require major restructuring of students' prior conceptions. Analogies can play a central role in this restructuring of students' conceptual framework. By activating prior knowledge, which has already been understood by the learner, the analogy helps students give meaning to incoming information."

—Mustafa Baser and Ömer Geban, *Effectiveness in Conceptual Change Instruction on Understanding of Heat and Temperature Concepts*

"Which of these things is not like the others?" For anyone who has watched *Sesame Street*, this question probably brings back happy memories of observing how various things are similar and different. Identifying similarities and differences helps learners gain insight, draw inferences, make generalizations, and develop or refine schemas (Holyoak, 2005). In addition, when students are presented with appropriately arranged contrasts, they are likely to notice new features they hadn't noticed previously and to learn which of those features are relevant to a particular concept (Bransford et al., 2000).

There are four strategies in the Identifying Similarities and Differences category, and we define each as follows:

- **Comparing** is the process of identifying similarities between or among things or ideas. The term *contrasting* refers to the process of identifying differences; most educators, however, use the term *comparing* to refer to both.
- **Classifying** is the process of organizing things into groups and labeling them according to their similarities.

- **Creating metaphors** is the process of identifying a general or basic pattern in a specific topic and then finding another topic that appears to be quite different but has the same general pattern.
- **Creating analogies** is the process of identifying relationships between pairs of concepts—identifying relationships between relationships.

These strategies help move students from existing knowledge to new knowledge, concrete to abstract, and separate to connected ideas. Students use what they already know as an anchor for new learning. As a result, many people consider these strategies to be the core of all learning (e.g., Bransford et al., 2000; Chen, 1999; Fuchs et al., 2006; Gentner, Loewenstein, & Thompson, 2003; Holyoak, 2005).

## Why This Category Is Important

Identifying similarities and differences is the process of comparing information, sorting concepts into categories, and making connections to existing knowledge. Simply put, identifying similarities and differences helps us make sense of the world. We ask, "Is this like that?" By answering the question, we enhance our existing mental representation or abstract schema for the information. This increases the likelihood that we will make connections to the schema when we encounter more new information and be able to make sense of that information.

How powerful is this strategy? The 12 studies included in the 2010 study produced an average effect size of 0.66, which is equivalent to a 25 percentile point gain. The first edition of this text reported an average effect size of 1.61 for identifying similarities and differences. Both sets of results indicate that teaching students how to identify similarities and differences is a worthwhile use of instructional time. The difference in effect sizes may reflect the smaller sample size or various methodological decisions the McREL researchers made in conducting the 2010 study.

For the research included in this study, effect sizes for identifying similarities and differences are highest when compared to a control group that received textbook-guided instruction. When the control group received intellectually engaging, interactive instruction, the effects of having students identify similarities and differences are the same as control group effects. In the set of studies included in the 2010 synthesis, activation of prior knowledge alone—without addressing connections between new and prior knowledge—is associated with mid-range and lower effect sizes (e.g., Ling, Chik, & Pang, 2006; Schwartz et al., 2006). In addition, asking students to generate analogies without guidance or teacher modeling is associated with a near-zero effect size (BouJaoude & Tamin, 1998). Interventions that include opportunities for reflection and group discussion show larger effect sizes (Baser & Geban, 2007; Chen, 1999; Mbajiorgu, Ezechi, & Idoko, 2007; Rule & Furletti, 2004).

One study included in the 2010 meta-analysis, which demonstrated one of the highest effect sizes, involved students' use of analogous problems to construct four problem-type schema. The intervention combined explicit instruction with structured practice, self-assessment, and prompting. The average effect size for this study was 2.05 (Fuchs et al., 2006).

What seems to be most effective is the practice of embedding this strategy as part of an instructional sequence that includes activating prior knowledge, introducing new knowledge, asking students to connect new and previous learning by identifying similarities and differences, and asking students to apply and demonstrate their understanding (Mbajiorgu et al., 2007; Rule & Furletti, 2004). Additional practices that facilitate student learning tie into McREL's research on other strategies, including providing supporting cues (e.g., posters of problem features, prompts for reflection, labeled diagrams), prompting students to reflect, and providing corrective feedback until students demonstrate understanding and proficiency.

The findings from the 2010 study are reflected in the work of other researchers. For example, Garner's (2007) work shows that teaching students to classify to make connections helps them rediscover forgotten information. Garner advises teachers to encourage their students to be conscious of how they process and remember information. Gentner (2003) and other researchers at Northwestern University found that novice learners either fail to make connections to previous knowledge or do so only at a superficial level, lending support to our recommendation to scaffold the process of identifying similarities and differences for students and provide them with aids such as graphic organizers.

# Classroom Practice for Identifying Similarities and Differences

The recommendations for classroom practice emphasize various ways of identifying similarities and differences and reflect the importance of teachers' guiding students in the process of identifying similarities and differences. There are three recommendations for classroom practice:

- Teach students a variety of ways to identify similarities and differences.
- Guide students as they engage in the process of identifying similarities and differences.
- Provide supporting cues to help students identify similarities and differences.

## Teach students a variety of ways to identify similarities and differences

The word *teach* here is significant. Similar to other higher-order thinking processes, students benefit from explicit instruction in the use of processes associated with identifying similarities and differences. This instruction should include providing students with steps in the process and modeling the process. Using a familiar context and familiar content when you model a process makes it possible for students to focus on that process—in other words, they don't have to think about understanding the content in addition to the process. After seeing the process modeled, students need multiple opportunities to practice it with corrective feedback (see Chapter 1). This allows students to shape and form their skills and develop automaticity with the process. Similarly, as we know from the research on nonlinguistic representation, providing students with graphic organizers for the processes associated with identifying similarities and differences helps them understand and carry out the critical elements of those processes. Graphic organizers help students categorize and make sense of what they are learning. Similarly, asking students to represent similarities and differences in symbolic form enhances their understanding and use of content.

Another important word in this practice is *variety*. We described four processes for identifying similarities and differences: comparing, classifying, creating metaphors, and creating analogies. Each of these processes offers students opportunities to think and learn at a deep level. Teachers generally are most familiar with and tend to engage students in comparing and classifying. We also encourage the use of metaphors and analogies, even with young students, because they provide rich learning experiences. In short, to maximize the benefits of identifying similarities and differences, teachers should provide students with multiple opportunities to use all four processes. In the sections that follow, we provide steps for each of the four processes and examples of how each might be used in the classroom.

**Comparing**

Comparing might seem like a simple process, but if done effectively, it involves some sophisticated thinking. The following steps illustrate what is involved with the process of comparing.

1. Select the items you want to compare.
2. Identify characteristics of the items on which to base your comparison.
3. Explain how the items are similar to and different from one another, with respect to the characteristics you identified.

### Example

Ms. Sedinger is helping her 6th grade students become more proficient at taking notes, which is a skill emphasized in the the 6th grade language arts standards ("Students take notes to enhance listening comprehension"). For several lessons, she provides teacher-prepared notes for students to use as she orally describes events from the Lewis and Clark expedition. One day, she helps students learn to use combination notes. The next day, as a way to help students deepen their understanding of the two types of note taking, she asks her students to compare the two types of notes.

Ms. Sedinger shows students how to use two different graphic organizers when comparing items: the Venn diagram and the comparison matrix. She explains that students should use a Venn diagram to compare one characteristic between two items. She emphasizes that similarities between the items are placed in the intersection of the two circles, and differences are placed in the respective nonintersecting parts of the circles. She then introduces the comparison matrix as another graphic organizer students can use when comparing two or more items on several characteristics at once. The students find the comparison matrix more challenging, so Ms. Sedinger knows she needs to provide more detailed directions to guide students when they are asked to compare items on several characteristics.

She begins by listing several characteristics of different types of notes, such as organization and use of symbols or pictures. Next, she asks students to select one characteristic and work with partners to compare informal outlining with combination notes, based on that one characteristic. Tom and Emiliano select the characteristic of organization. They use a Venn diagram to list how the two types of notes are similar and different (Figure 8.1).

---

FIGURE 8.1
Example of Venn Diagram

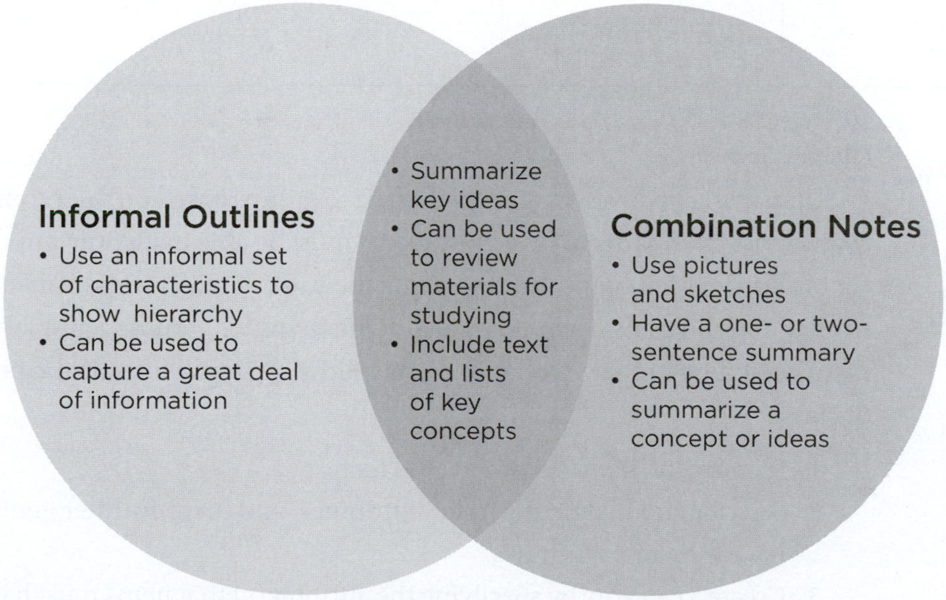

**Informal Outlines**
- Use an informal set of characteristics to show hierarchy
- Can be used to capture a great deal of information

- Summarize key ideas
- Can be used to review materials for studying
- Include text and lists of key concepts

**Combination Notes**
- Use pictures and sketches
- Have a one- or two-sentence summary
- Can be used to summarize a concept or ideas

After students complete their Venn diagrams, Ms. Sedinger combines the class information and places it in a comparison matrix (Figure 8.2). This helps her students better understand how to use a comparison matrix and shows them that if they are confused by the comparison matrix, they can start with a Venn diagram and compare items one characteristic at a time. By scaffolding the process for students and providing them with graphic organizers, Ms. Sedinger helps her students gradually acquire key lifelong learning skills in dealing with information at a high level.

FIGURE 8.2

**Example of a Comparison Matrix**

|  | **Uses graphics** | **Captures a large amount of information** | **Good for summarizing** |
|---|---|---|---|
| **Combination Notes** | X |  | X |
| **Informal Outlines** |  | X |  |

## Classifying

Classifying involves organizing items into groups based on their common characteristics. In order to classify, students must be able to identify important characteristics of an item and determine the ways in which various items are similar and different. Then they classify the items by grouping and labeling them according to their similarities. The following steps illustrate the process of classifying:

1. Identify the items you want to classify.
2. Select an item, describe its key attributes, and identify other items that have the same attributes.
3. Create a category by specifying the attribute(s) that items must have for membership in this category.

4. Select another item, describe its key attributes, and identify other items that have the same attributes.

5. Create a second category by specifying the attribute(s) that items must have for membership in the category.

6. Repeat the previous two steps until all items are classified and the specific attributes have been identified for membership in each category.

7. If necessary, combine categories or split them into smaller categories, and specify attribute(s) that determine membership in each category.

To help students learn the classifying process, teachers can provide the categories initially. When students are more familiar with the process, they can create the categories into which items are classified. Students should be able to explain why a particular item belongs to a category and be able to reclassify the same set of items, focusing on a different attribute. Using a circle or chart graphic organizer to record how they classify items supports students' understanding of the content being classified (see Downloadable Figure 7).

## Example

Mrs. Hernandez's 12th grade English class is studying common themes in literature and working on the state standard that requires students to know the defining characteristics of a variety of literary forms and genres. Her students are surprised and even skeptical when she states that many people believe there are only 12 themes that encompass almost all books, movies, and plays.

She asks her students to create a list on the board of their favorite books, movies, and television shows. She then presents them with the 12 common themes in literature and asks them to work in groups to match the movies, books, and television shows they selected to the appropriate theme (and determine if there were any that don't fit neatly into one or more themes). Finally, Mrs. Hernandez asks her students to use a graphic organizer to classify and organize the movies, books, and shows (see Downloadable Figure 8).

Mrs. Hernandez could have presented the 12 themes to her students and given them an example of each. Instead, she intentionally uses the strategy of classification to encourage her students to make personal connections to the material and think critically about the subject. Using classification in this manner provides students with a robust learning experience.

### Creating Metaphors

A metaphor is a powerful tool when trying to provide students with an anchor for new learning, especially when that new learning might be an abstract or difficult-to-understand idea. For example, when the Internet was new, it was difficult for many people to grasp the idea that information was "darting around in thin air." When experts began to metaphorically refer to the Internet as an "information superhighway," we had an anchor for developing our understanding about the Internet. We understand that a superhighway is a fast way to travel from point A to point B. We know that superhighways have on ramps and off ramps and when traffic is heavy, travel is slow. We also understand that the going is not always easy. Sometimes traffic is heavy, there are bumps in the road, we get lost, or the road is closed. This mental image of a superhighway, based on our own experiences, allowed many of us to develop a basic understanding of how the Internet works.

Metaphors can be used in all content areas to help students make sense of information. Teachers should intentionally plan to use metaphors when they want students to focus on how items are similar on an abstract level (Harrison & De Jong, 2005). Used appropriately, metaphors make it easy for students to connect what they don't know to what they already do know. To realize the power of metaphors, teachers must first teach what metaphors are and how to create them. Teachers must also help students understand that a metaphor connects two items at an abstract, nonliteral, level. The steps for creating a metaphor, graphic organizers for representing metaphors, and examples of how teachers might use the creating metaphors strategy follow (see also Downloadable Figure 9).

1. Identify the basic or most important elements of the information or situation with which you are working.
2. Write that basic information as a more general pattern by

- Replacing words for specific things with words for more general things.
- Summarizing information whenever possible.

3. Find new information or situations to which the general pattern applies.

## Example

Ms. Daigneault's kindergarten students are sitting in front of her as she reads the story *A Rainbow in Our Garden*. The story is about a little boy and girl who plant seeds that grow into beautiful flowers that match the colors of the rainbow. There are red petunias, orange poppies, yellow daisies, and so on. When Ms. Daigneault finishes reading the story, she says, "The title of the book is *A Rainbow in Our Garden*. Do we plant seeds in the sky?" The children giggle and emphatically answer, "No!" She then asks, "Then how can we have a rainbow in our garden?"

The students excitedly explain that the flowers are all different colors, so the garden looks like a rainbow. Ms. Daigneault tells them they are correct and then explains that when something reminds us of something else because those two things are alike in some ways, we are using a metaphor. She explains that when the children in the story see the colorful flowers growing in their garden, they say the flowers remind them of a beautiful rainbow they saw in the sky.

**Creating Analogies**

An analogy helps us see similarities between things that seem dissimilar on the surface. It expresses the relationship between two pairs of items. A familiar format for analogies is A:B::C:D (read as "*A* is to *B* as *C* is to *D*"). For example, in the analogy *hot:cold::night:day,* the relationship between night and day is the same as the relationship between hot and cold: they are opposites. Students sometimes find analogies challenging because they involve relationships between relationships. In this example, students first have to figure out the relationship between *hot* and *cold* and then identify another pair of items that has the same relationship. One of the pairs in an analogy should be familiar, whereas the other is the target to be learned or understood. Analogies are useful for learning because if students know and understand the relationship between one of the pairs of items in the analogy, they can better understand the relationship between the other pair of items. Students can use a graphic organizer to represent analogies of the A:B::C:D form (see Downloadable Figure 10).

The steps for creating an analogy are

1. Identify how the two items in the first pair are related.
2. State the relationship in a general way.
3. Identify another pair of items that share a similar relationship.

Using the A:B::C:D format for analogies is one way to help students develop an understanding of new ideas or concepts. Another approach is to create an analogous situation. Keith Holyoak writes, "Two situations are analogous if they share a common pattern of relationships among their constituent elements even though the elements themselves differ across the two situations" (2005, p. 117). For example, when Charles Darwin was trying to explain his theory of natural selection, he employed the example of farmers using specific breeding techniques to produce desired breeds of livestock and plants. Because people had some familiarity with agricultural breeding, it was easier to conceptualize the idea of natural selection.

Analogies are very powerful teaching and learning devices. As with metaphors, it is important to intentionally plan for the use of this strategy. This means identifying where an analogy would be a good strategy to anchor learning and specifying the analogy that will be shared with students. It is difficult for most people to create analogies on the spot, so it is important to take time to identify or create appropriate analogies. As you read the following example, notice how the teacher intentionally plans for the use of an analogy.

### Example

Ms. Hanson, a 5th grade teacher, is wrapping up a social studies unit on the 1960s. The class has just finished studying the impact of the Kennedy presidency on space exploration. She asks her class to use the vast amount of material they studied in this unit to complete the following analogy, which she represents with a graphic organizer: "JFK's 'We choose to go to the moon' speech is to space exploration as . . ."

Students work in groups of two or three to identify the relationship between the first pair of items and to think of a good example that would complete the analogy. Some of their responses include

- "as Martin Luther King Jr's 'I have a dream' speech is to the Civil Rights movement."
- "as Woodstock is to the antiestablishment, hippy movement."
- "as the Kent State shootings are to the end of the Vietnam War."

Ms. Hanson then invites the groups to share their reasoning for why they chose their analogies. After all of the groups share their analogies, she asks students to write in their journals about what they now understand about the 1960s as a result of this analogy activity. Although Ms. Hanson might not agree with all of the analogies, she is very pleased that students understand the concept that a major event or speech is linked to a movement that lasts much longer than the event itself. As with metaphors, the deep thinking that happens during these classroom discussions is a powerful indicator of student understanding.

## Guide students as they engage in the process of identifying similarities and differences

Presenting students with explicit guidance in identifying similarities and differences enhances their understanding of and ability to use knowledge. Teachers can take a direct approach to providing guidance by simply stating the similarities and differences between items. This approach is effective when teachers provide opportunities for students to actively participate in discussions about the similarities and differences and ask questions about them.

Teachers can also guide students in identifying similarities and differences by providing them with structured tasks. For teacher-directed comparison tasks, teachers identify items to compare and characteristics on which to base the comparison. These types of tasks focus the conclusions that students draw and are used when all students should obtain a general awareness of the same similarities and differences for the same characteristics. For teacher-directed classification tasks, teachers provide elements to be classified and categories into which they should be classified. The focus for these tasks is on placing items into their appropriate categories and understanding why they belong in those categories.

It might be necessary to provide students with a number of teacher-directed tasks before they are comfortable creating their own metaphors and analogies. For teacher-directed metaphors, teachers provide the first element of the metaphor and the abstract relationship. For teacher-directed analogies, there are two options. Teachers might provide a complete analogy and ask students to explain how the relationship between one pair of items is similar to the relationship between the other pair of items, or teachers might present an analogy that is missing one item and ask students to identify that item.

There is also a strong research base that supports the effectiveness of having students identify similarities and differences without direct input from the teacher (e.g., Chen, 1999). As students become more familiar with each process, teachers should provide opportunities for them to do so independently, gradually removing the scaffolding provided by teacher-directed tasks. Teachers can use student-directed tasks to stimulate divergence in students' thinking. When comparison tasks are student directed, students select the characteristics on which items are compared or select both items to be compared as well as the characteristics on which they base that comparison. Similarly, student-directed classification tasks provide opportunities for students to form the categories into which a given set of items will be sorted or to select items to be sorted and their appropriate categories.

For student-directed metaphors, students might be given one element of a metaphor and asked to identify the second element and then describe the abstract relationship. Student-directed analogy tasks ask students to provide more than one element of an analogy. It is important to provide students with opportunities to reflect on and discuss their comparisons, classifications, analogies, and metaphors, whether they are working with teacher-directed or student-directed tasks (Wittrock & Alesandrini, 1990). It is especially critical that they do this for the metaphors and analogies they create as part of student-directed tasks so teachers can check the students' understanding of the content for any misconceptions and ensure that students extended their learning as a result of the task rather than focused on trivial aspects of the content.

Teacher guidance should also come in the form of corrective feedback. Providing structured learning opportunities with focused feedback during teacher-directed and student-directed tasks will help students hone their skills and build their confidence with identifying similarities and differences. As students gain skills and confidence, teachers can gradually provide less structure and more opportunities for students to provide their own feedback. Ultimately, students should be able to identify similarities and differences on their own, using the appropriate process for a given situation.

### Example

Ms. Bedoin explains to her 4th grade students that metaphors often are used to help people understand new or abstract concepts by presenting unfamiliar information in a familiar context. She shares several examples of metaphors (e.g., a paragraph is a sandwich of sentences) and poses questions that help her students understand the abstract relationship represented by the metaphors. Next, she provides students with one element of a metaphor and the abstract relationship, and she then asks students to identify the other element. She provides students with opportunities to practice using metaphors in mathematics class by asking them to select one of their vocabulary words and create a metaphor that will help other students better understand the term. During the year, she provides less and less scaffolding for students as they use and create metaphors to understand new information and concepts.

## Provide supporting cues to help students identify similarities and differences

In the 2010 study, teachers in the more effective interventions (those that directly addressed identifying similarities and differences) provided additional support to students by directing their attention to important features of the targeted knowledge (Baser & Geban, 2007; Fuchs et al., 2006; Pang & Marton, 2005; Rule & Furletti, 2004; Schwartz et al., 2006; Walton & Walton, 2002). They did this by providing posters of important problem features, labeled diagrams, and prompts that helped students reflect on what they were learning. Other ways to provide supportive cues are to point out patterns in information (e.g., similar spelling patterns among vocabulary words, steps in processes, parts of a system), provide a set of guiding questions to help students understand a metaphor (e.g., How are the two elements of the metaphor the same?), or use everyday objects as analogs (e.g., the plumbing in a house as an analog for the circulatory system).

### Example

Mr. Kendall's 8th graders are studying the respiratory and circulatory systems. To help his students remember the key components of those systems, he places detailed posters of the systems around the classroom. The posters serve as reminders about the important components of each system and help students understand the relationships among the various parts of the systems. Students then create metaphors for each system and find pictures to represent their metaphors. Mr. Kendall posts the pictures as additional reminders about the components of each system. For example, Jake creates a metaphor using a barge on a river. The barge (red blood cells) moves through the water (blood stream) exchanging cargo. Good materials (oxygen) are deposited at various sites, and garbage (carbon dioxide) is carried away.

## Identifying Similarities and Differences with Today's Learners

McREL released a study in 1998 (Marzano & Kendall, 1998) that found it would take 22 years, on average, for a student to learn all of the concepts listed in a typical K–12 curriculum, far beyond the 13 years we generally give students! Our curricula often are a "mile wide and an inch thick." There is so much content that teachers can teach few topics in depth. If a district develops a guaranteed and viable curriculum, then teachers should be able to teach the content to the appropriate level of knowledge in the allotted time. Nevertheless, there will always be more to learn about a topic than can be covered during school hours.

With new information and content being created and made accessible every day, we are not likely to accomplish the task of "covering" all there is to know about a particular topic, nor should it even be our goal to do so. Instead, students need to learn skills that allow them to apply existing concepts to new and unfamiliar situations, moving beyond "right-answer learning" toward application of learning. The processes outlined in this chapter help teachers provide these opportunities to students.

Consider Katie, for example, a high school student who has started working part time at a local computer and electronics store. One day, as she helps a customer choose his first laptop, she finds herself struggling to explain the difference between RAM and storage memory. Remembering how the process of metaphors helped her understand complex issues in her classes, she draws upon this skill to help her customer.

"Imagine your physical office. You have a desk or a table where you can work on your active projects. You also likely have a file cabinet where you can keep your documents and other things that you aren't working on right at the moment."

When the customer confirms, Katie goes on: "The larger your table or desk is, the more projects you can take out at once and spread across your workspace. That's your RAM; you can have more programs running and documents open at once without slowing down your computer. Think of your filing cabinet as the storage memory. The larger your filing cabinet, the more projects you can have filed on your computer. For example, I enjoy working with multimedia, making videos, and creating original music on my computer, all while my browser and social networking applications are running, so I'd need a 'large table,' or lots of RAM. However, if you're mostly going to be checking e-mail, surfing the net, and using a word processor, you don't need nearly as much RAM."

The customer smiles as he begins to understand and Katie eventually helps him pick out a laptop with the right specifications for the work he will be doing. Ultimately, identifying similarities and differences not only helps Katie make connections for herself as a learner but also helps her explain confusing concepts to others.

## Tips for Teaching Using Identifying Similarities and Differences

1. Select the strategy that best fits the learning experience.

- Use comparing when you want students to identify how items are similar and different.
- Use classifying when you want students to place items in categories and understand why items belong in those categories.
- Use metaphors when you want students to focus on how items are similar on an abstract level.
- Use analogies when you want students to understand abstract ideas and make connections between new knowledge and prior knowledge by using what they know about the relationship between a set of known items.

2. Provide students with graphic organizers that best represent the relevant process for identifying similarities and differences.
   - For comparing, use Venn diagrams or comparison matrices.
   - For classifying, use a chart or circle diagram.
   - For metaphors, use a chart or metaphor pattern diagram.
   - For analogies, use a pictorial form of the A:B::C:D format.

3. Provide opportunities for students to develop their own graphic organizers to use for each of the approaches to identifying similarities and differences.

4. Ensure that students understand the process of comparing before asking them to classify.

5. Model each of the processes for identifying similarities and differences multiple times. Include corrective feedback as students practice the processes and use the associated graphic organizers. Set the stage for students to provide their own feedback.

6. Explicitly name a process as students use it in class. If a student uses a metaphor as part of an explanation, state to the class that the student has used a metaphor. The more opportunities students have to view or experience the four processes throughout the day, and in multiple academic settings, the more likely it is they will develop deep understanding of content and use the processes frequently.

7. Ask students to explain their thinking as they compare, classify, create metaphors, and create analogies.

# 9

# Generating and Testing Hypotheses

"What if *Brown v. Board of Education* had been decided in favor of the Board of Education of Topeka? What if Mark Twain had written *Adventures of Huckleberry Finn* from Jim's perspective? What if the rules of baseball were changed so that batters were out after two strikes? What if the federal government provided no support to public education?"

What is there about "what if" questions that grab our attention? Robert Cialdini (2005) argues that such questions tap into our natural inclination to solve problems. Mysteries, puzzles, and problems make us think about everyday occurrences from different perspectives and require critical thinking skills. As students answer these questions, they draw upon their knowledge to generate and test hypotheses—they make and test predictions, consider various options, and draw conclusions. In the process, they elaborate on their understanding of that knowledge and their ability to apply it and connect to the real-life purposes behind the content and skills they are learning.

The questions posed at the beginning of this chapter demonstrate that generating and testing hypotheses isn't something that only happens in science class, for example. The mental processes involved in asking questions and seeking answers can occur in all content areas (e.g., Bottge, Rueda, & Skivington, 2006; Simons & Klein, 2007; Ward & Lee, 2004). We might refer to hypothesizing by different names in other content areas—predicting, inferring, deducing, or theorizing—but the mental processes used are the same. To underscore this point, we present several types of structured tasks that can be used to provide students with opportunities to generate and test hypotheses in various content areas.

## Why This Category Is Important

Generating and testing hypotheses applies knowledge by using two thinking processes that can be used alone or in tandem with each other. One of these processes is deduction, which involves using general rules to make a prediction about a future event or action. People use deductive reasoning naturally in everyday situations. For example, when students begin to read a story about a turtle, they naturally access some of the generalizations they have about turtles from their permanent memory. If one of those generalizations is "Turtles use their shells to protect themselves from predators," then they will likely predict that the story will include some information about the turtle hiding in its shell when threatened by another animal or a human.

Similarly, students apply general rules related to content. For example, when students know that earthquakes occur along geologic fault lines, they can make predictions about where other earthquakes might occur, based on observations of these same geologic conditions in various parts of the world. Students need a depth of knowledge about a topic or subject area to make and use generalizations to generate and test hypotheses. To ensure that students have the knowledge they need, the curriculum must include specific attention to generalizations and principles in the various content areas and the conditions under which they apply.

Induction, the second thinking process, involves making inferences that are based on knowledge that students already have or information that is presented to them. Induction involves drawing new conclusions or identifying rules based on observations or patterns in information. Compare this to deductive thinking, which involves applying a generalization or rule that is known or provided to the student. For example, when students read a story and infer why the main character took a specific action, they use inductive reasoning. Inductive reasoning helps students use what they know about a situation to "read between the lines" and figure out things that are not explicitly stated. It also helps them increase their ability to make connections and see patterns in the information available, both inside and outside the classroom.

Generally speaking, deductive approaches produce better results than inductive approaches. The inductive approach provides students with opportunities to discover principles and generalizations on their own, but it also provides opportunities for students to stray from the main questions and primary learning tasks. Misconceptions can easily form as students, investigating on their own, create an incomplete or incorrect understanding. Teachers who do not realize that misconceptions can be a byproduct of induction often fail to "unearth" the inaccuracies in students' understanding. This does not mean that the inductive approach is not a good teaching strategy. It means that to use the inductive approach effectively, teachers must have a solid understanding of the content, debrief inductive learning experiences with students, and provide formative assessment opportunities to ensure that students have not developed or reinforced misconceptions as they constructed their own meaning from the instruction. The deductive approach provides students with a more complete learning framework. Fewer misconceptions are formed, and students still have opportunities to investigate and explore.

Generating and testing hypotheses deepens students' knowledge because it requires the use of critical thinking skills such as analysis and evaluation. These processes also motivate students by accessing their natural inclination to solve problems. The overall effect size for the 15 studies analyzed in the 2010 study is 0.25. For the most rigorous experimental studies (11 of 15 studies), the average effect size of 0.58 was similar to the overall effect size of 0.61 that was reported in the first edition of *Classroom Instruction That Works*.

Generating and testing hypotheses is particularly effective when compared to more traditional instructional activities, such as lectures and teacher-directed, step-by-step activities. For example, Ward and Lee (2004) find that students who are involved in problem-based learning in a high school nutrition class, which involves students generating and testing possible solutions to real-life problems, have a better understanding of the connections among the content, their own personal lives, and the work world than students taught using a lecture-based approach. Other studies indicate that when students generate and test hypotheses by engaging in problem solving, they ultimately have a clearer understanding of lesson concepts (e.g., Hsu, 2008; Rivet & Krajcik, 2004; Tarhan & Acar, 2007). For example, in the study by Tarhan and Acar (2007), students in a chemistry class who learn through a lecture-based approach form alternative conceptions about intermolecular forces, whereas students who learn through a problem-based approach do not. Engaging in activities that involve generating and testing hypotheses also helps students make connections between academic content and real-world situations, such as improving air quality in their communities, preventing the spread of communicable diseases, and using machines to construct large buildings (Marx et al., 2004; Rivet & Krajcik, 2004).

## Classroom Practice for Generating and Testing Hypotheses

Although we often think of generating and testing hypotheses as a task for science class, students can engage in this process in all content areas. When students create thesis statements, make predictions based on evidence, or ask "If I do this, what might happen?" they are using the process of generating and testing hypotheses. There are two recommendations for classroom practice:

- Engage students in a variety of structured tasks for generating and testing hypotheses.
- Ask students to explain their hypotheses and their conclusions.

### Engage students in a variety of structured tasks for generating and testing hypotheses

A variety of tasks helps provide a context for students to generate and test hypotheses. These tasks include processes such as systems analysis, problem solving, experimental inquiry, and investigation. Two other processes, decision making and invention, were included in the first edition of *Classroom Instruction That Works*. For this edition, the basic aspects of these processes have been incorporated into problem solving. For example, as students complete the steps of problem solving, they must determine which solution is best. Invention requires the determination of a solution to meet a specific need or make improvements, a process that is similar to overcoming the constraints in a problem.

To ensure students' success with tasks that involve each of these processes, teachers should

- Model the processes for students.
- Use familiar content to teach the steps of the processes.
- Provide students with useful and relevant graphic organizers.
- Give students guidance as needed.

To maximize students' learning, teachers should relate the learning embedded in tasks using these processes to students' existing knowledge, previous experience, and interests (Schroeder et al., 2007).

As teachers intentionally incorporate these four processes into lesson design and delivery, they provide opportunities for students to employ critical thinking skills, to work collaboratively with peers, and to engage in discourse as they describe their learning and thinking. Explicit use of each of these processes equips students with a mechanism for extending and applying their knowledge. Brief definitions and the steps of these four processes follow.

**Systems analysis**

Systems analysis is the process of analyzing the parts of a system and the manner in which they interact. The steps in the process of systems analysis are

- Explain the purpose of the system, the parts of the system, and the function of each part.
- Describe how the parts affect one another.
- Identify a part of the system, describe a change in that part, and then hypothesize what would happen as a result of this change.
- When possible, test your hypothesis by actually changing the part or by using a simulation to change the part.

### Example

Mr. Jonas, a high school social studies teacher, wants to show how various practices led to the collapse of the housing market during the recession of the late 2000s. To demonstrate, he sets up a two-day simulation in which students "sell" their desks to peers, who easily qualify for loans much larger than they can actually afford. The students who clean up their desks and move them to the sunny side of the room enjoy seeing that they can charge much more for their desks than other students can charge.

Midway through the simulation, Mr. Jonas informs some of the students that they have lost their jobs and can no longer continue making mortgage payments to the bank. The class quickly realizes that the banks are no longer able to give loans, since they aren't getting paid by lenders. Some students realize that they overpaid for a simple desk.

Mr. Jonas asks students to form groups of three and identify different parts of the economic system and how they interacted in the simulation. He also challenges students to propose a change in one part of the system and predict what might happen to the other parts of the system if that change were made. Using this simulation, Mr. Jonas helps his students see how a few changes to an economic system can wreak havoc on the system as a whole.

### Problem solving

Problem solving involves overcoming constraints or limiting conditions that are in the way of achieving goals. The steps in problem solving include the following:

- Identify the goal you are trying to accomplish.
- Describe the barriers or constraints that are preventing you from achieving your goal or are creating the problem.
- Identify different solutions for overcoming the barriers or constraints and hypothesize which solution is likely to work.
- Try your solution, either in reality or through a simulation.
- Explain whether your hypothesis was correct. Determine if you want to test another hypothesis using a different solution. In some cases, this may involve building or designing an invention.

## Example

South Valley Middle School wants to hold its spring band concert in spite of losing some important instruments during a flood that occurred when a pipe in the building burst.

"We will need to find ways to overcome a very big problem," says Mr. Schneider. "We no longer have a bass drum to help us keep a steady beat during the songs."

Kyle says, "We can use the cymbals to keep a steady beat."

Marco says, "I can play one note on my tuba over and over again in a steady pattern."

Jan, who thinks her idea is better than any presented so far, says, "Susan and I can clap our hands, and that will set and keep the rhythm."

Raul suggests they try hitting a plastic pickle tub with a bass drum stick to keep the beat.

Mr. Schneider is pleased that his students have so many ideas and are ready to step forward to solve the problem. "Let's look at each of the suggested solutions, determine the pros and cons of each, and try them out," says Mr. Schneider. "Which of the ideas do you all believe will best solve our problem?" Students discuss the barriers to each of the proposed ideas and then make predictions about what might happen when each of the solutions is tested.

"Well, let's see what happens," says Mr. Schneider. First, the band plays while Kyle and Kelly tap the cymbals together. The boys are able to keep a steady beat, but the cymbals vibrate and make noises that distract from the songs. Next, Marco plays a note over and over again on his tuba. Again, just like Kyle and Kelly, Marco is able to keep a steady beat, but by playing just one note there are times when his playing seems out of tune with the song. Jan and Susan stand in front of the band and loudly clap their hands, keeping a steady rhythm. Although their hands are a little sore, the girls do a nice job of keeping a constant beat. Finally, Raul uses his bass drum stick to hit the plastic pickle tub, which he got from the school cafeteria. Although it is clear that he is hitting plastic, the sound isn't too bad and the beat can be heard.

After trying the four solutions, the students discuss what happened with the cymbals, the tuba, the hand clapping, and the plastic tub. Although each of the solutions accomplished the needed outcome, each also had certain drawbacks. After reviewing the outcomes, the students agree that the best solution for their short performance at the concert is to have Raul use the plastic pickle tub.

Mr. Schneider congratulates his students on their good thinking and explains that they employed the strategy of problem solving. They took the problem of not having a bass drum, came up with several possible solutions, predicted the success of each solution, experimented to determine the actual results, and selected the solution that best solved the problem. In the end, the spring band concert was a success.

### Experimental inquiry

Experimental inquiry is the process of generating and testing explanations of observed phenomena. The steps in experimental inquiry include the following:

- Observe something of interest to you and describe what you observe.
- Apply specific theories or rules to what you have observed.
- Based on your explanation, generate a hypothesis to predict what would happen if you applied the theories or rules to what you observed or to a situation related to what you observed.
- Set up an experiment or engage in an activity to test your hypothesis.
- Explain the results of your experiment or activity. Decide if your hypothesis was correct and if you need to conduct additional experiments or activities or if you need to generate and test an alternative hypothesis.

## Example

Ms. Alexander is working with her 4th grade class on the benchmark objective about changes to Earth's surface caused by slow and rapid processes (e.g., weathering, erosion, landslides, volcanic eruptions). During this lesson, her goal is to have students understand how water flowing down a slope can cause erosion and how the angle of the slope affects the amount of erosion. She begins by asking students to think about water and how it carries away debris in the street during and after a heavy rain. She then asks them to form groups and discuss other examples of how flowing water changes their backyards, the playground, and the areas next to the creek behind the school. After students share their examples, Ms. Alexander asks them to think about how the effects of a heavy rain and a light rain are different.

She then explains that they will pour water down an erosion tray, positioned at different angles, to investigate the relationship between the angle of the tray and the amount of erosion. Pairs of students begin the experiment by writing predictions about how the angle of the erosion tray affects the amount of erosion, as measured by the sediment that collects in the tray. Ashley and Juan predict that the amount of sediment will be the same in each case, because the amount of water and the speed of flow stay the same. Amos and Brittany predict that the steeper the angle, the more sediment will be washed away by the stream of water. After writing their predictions, students conduct two trials. They allow one gallon of water to flow down the erosion tray and then record the angle of the tray and the amount of sediment in the tray. Next, they set up a second erosion tray at a steeper angle. The same amount of water flows down the erosion tray at the same rate, and students once again record the amount of sediment in the tray.

Following the second trial, Ms. Alexander asks the pairs to move into groups of four and discuss their results. Ashley and Juan see that their prediction was wrong. Amos and Brittany see their prediction confirmed—as the angle increases, so does the amount of sediment. After the discussion, students write the results of the experiment in their science journals, along with an explanation of why their hypotheses were confirmed or disproven.

## Investigation

Investigation is the process of identifying and resolving issues regarding past events about which there are confusions or contradictions. The steps in the investigation process include the following:

- Clearly identify the situation (i.e., concept to be defined, historical event to be explained, hypothetical future event to be defined or explained).
- Identify what is already known or agreed upon.
- Offer a hypothetical scenario, based on what you understand and know about the situation.
- Seek out and analyze evidence to determine if your hypothetical scenario is plausible.

### Example

Mr. Burns's 8th grade history class is studying early European exploration and colonization of North America. He wants his students to understand how people's interpretations of early explorers' voyages and interactions with indigenous cultures have changed over time. He asks his students to think about how Christopher Columbus should be viewed through the lens of history. Can we say that Columbus "discovered" the new world if people were already living there? Was he even the first European explorer to visit the continent?

To encourage students to consider other perspectives, Mr. Burns shows a news clip that features American Indian groups protesting a Columbus Day parade and celebrations in a midwestern U.S. city. The story makes it clear that these American Indian groups view Columbus as the first in a long line of Europeans who came to take their lands and erase their culture. It also presents another point of view: Italian American groups in the city want to continue to celebrate Columbus's journey as a way of honoring their heritage and its influence on what is now the United States.

Mr. Burns tells his students that a bill has been proposed by their county government to ban celebrations of Columbus and eliminate paid holidays for government workers on Columbus Day. He organizes students into groups and assigns each group one of three positions to defend before the county commission:

1. Christopher Columbus was a brave and valiant explorer, and we should continue to honor his accomplishments with local celebrations and a government holiday.

2. Christopher Columbus did not discover America. He simply got lost. As a result, entire American Indian cultures were changed for the worse. We should not honor this man with parades and a government holiday.

3. We should continue to allow parades honoring Christopher Columbus, but there is no reason to provide a paid government holiday for county workers. Columbus was a brave explorer whose journey changed the world in many ways, some positive and some negative.

Mr. Burns asks the students defending position 1 to meet together, discuss their defense, and decide on the strongest arguments. Similarly, those who will defend positions 2 and 3 meet and prepare their arguments. As each group presents its argument, the other two groups serve as the county commission and give feedback about the presentation, using a rubric provided by Mr. Burns.

For homework, Mr. Burns asks students to write in their journals what they learned about different interpretations of explorers' voyages and interactions with indigenous cultures, as well as how their own thoughts changed as a result of constructing and listening to others' arguments for the various positions. Students share their reflections at the beginning of the next class.

## Ask students to explain their hypotheses and their conclusions

Asking students to explain the principles from which they work, the hypotheses they generate from these principles, and why their hypotheses make sense helps students deepen their understanding of the principles they are applying (Darling-Hammond et al., 2008; Lavoie, 1999; Lavoie & Good, 1988; Lawson, 1988; Pitler, Hubbell, Kuhn, & Malenoski, 2007; Tweed, 2009). If an inductive approach is employed, students will begin by making observations from which they will derive generalizations. Teachers might ask students to explain the logic underlying their observations, how their observations support their hypotheses, how their experiment tests their hypotheses, and how their results confirm or disprove their hypotheses. If a deductive technique were employed, students would not be engaged in the observation phase because they would begin with a generalization or principle that had been derived from previous observations.

Designing assignments that let students know they must be able to describe how they generated their hypotheses and explain what they learned as a result of testing helps students focus on these important aspects of the process and increases their ability to use the process. To accomplish this, teachers should

- Provide students with templates for reporting their work, highlighting the areas in which they are expected to provide explanations.
- Provide sentence frames for students (especially young students) that help them articulate their explanations.
- Ask students to create audio recordings in which they explain their hypotheses and conclusions.
- Provide or collaboratively develop rubrics that identify the criteria on which students will be evaluated.
- Provide opportunities for students to create graphic organizers that help them make sense of the material.
- Establish events at which parents or community members can ask students to explain their thinking.

The following example shows how a 2nd grade teacher designed activities that required students to explain how they generated and tested hypotheses.

## Example

Mrs. Lemmon and her class of 2nd graders have been working on skip-counting by 2s, 5s, and 10s. She now wishes to engage her students in identifying patterns when skip-counting by 9. Because these 2nd graders are preparing for future work with multiplication, it is less important that they memorize the numbers than it is that they recognize skip-counting can result in many fascinating patterns. Therefore, instead of explicitly teaching the patterns, she decides to use an inductive reasoning approach. In this way, students can discover for themselves the many patterns that exist in multiples of 9.

With students sitting in small groups, Mrs. Lemmon asks them to count out nine counters (e.g., small chips, slips of paper, tokens). She then asks the class to use a graphic organizer and record how many tens and how many units are represented. The students record 0 in the tens column and 9 in the units column (to represent a value of 9). She then asks students to repeat this process, continuing on from nine, and record the new values for each column: 1 in the tens column and 8 in the units column (to represent a value of 18). She does this with the class two more times. The students' graphic organizer is shown in Downloadable Figure 11.

Next, she asks students to put the counters away. "Take a close look at your table so far," she says to the class. "There are several patterns. Here is your task: Find a pattern and use that pattern to fill in the rest of the table."

Ella, Sean, and Armand are seated together at one table. Armand notices that each row adds up to 9. Ella answers, "Okay, so what are other ways to make 9? Let's see . . . 8 and 1 . . ."

Armand chimes in with "4 and 5 . . ."

Sean asks, "Can we do 5 and 4 also? Or do you think we can only list each number once?"

They decide that they can repeat numbers, since they learned in previous lessons that these represent number families. They begin filling in their table with addends of 9, such as "6 and 3" and "4 and 5." Although they successfully create multiples of 9, they are not in any particular order.

Audra, Jeffery, and Erika are at another table. Jeffery notes that the tens column counts up by 1. "Look! It goes 0, 1, 2, 3 . . . I bet the next number in that column is 4."

Audra agrees and also notices that the units column is counting backwards by 1. "So maybe the next number when counting by nines is 45." Using this pattern, the students fill in their chart.

Once the students have finished filling in their tables, Mrs. Lemmon asks them to verify their numbers by using the counters. Ella, Sean, and Armand notice that their numbers are correct but not in the right order. Mrs. Lemmon asks them to share how they found these numbers. Though the numbers are out of order, this group notices an important characteristic of multiples of 9: The sum of its digits will be 9. Audra, Jeffrey, and Erika's group correctly identified the multiples of 9, but they learned an additional "trick" from the previous group.

This lesson shows how experimental inquiry, with careful debriefing led by the teacher, can result in deep learning and understanding of concepts. It was important for Mrs. Lemmon to have her students verify their own hypotheses and then to bring the group back together at the end of the lesson to make certain that students were not forming misconceptions. Lessons such as these tend to be much more engaging and result in deeper understanding for her students than if Mrs. Lemmon had simply asked them to memorize the multiples of 9.

## Generating and Testing Hypotheses with Today's Learners

In the opening chapters, we make the case that limiting classroom activities to right-answer learning no longer serves students who have immediate access to a plethora of information. As Karl Fisch states, we are preparing students for jobs that don't exist yet, which will use technologies that haven't been invented yet, to solve problems we have not yet realized (Fisch & McLeod, 2007). What we ultimately want students to be able to do is find issues that are important to them, gather as much information as possible from a wide variety of resources that represent various viewpoints and motivations, and test—to the best of their abilities—the viability of these claims in order to inform their own decisions. By generating and testing hypotheses and by using the associated processes—systems analysis, problem solving, experimental inquiry, and investigation—students are able to develop these skills.

What may be most timely with this strategy in particular is the fact that social networking tools now exist to help us create our own microcommunities. This means we have methods not only to connect with friends and peers who have common interests but also to quickly sift through vast amounts of information and find what is relevant and interesting to us. There is, however, a downside to this. Because we can create our own microcommunities, it becomes very easy to live in echo chambers that broadcast only the opinions of like-minded individuals. To avoid this, teachers must encourage students to actively seek out different voices, opinions, and perspectives.

This idea is related to recent articles and blog posts about "new literacies" or "Literacy 2.0" (e.g., Frey, Fisher, & Gonzalez, 2010; Hubbell, 2009; Knobel & Wilber, 2009). At one time, literacy referred to the ability to read and understand information and to retell this information in a new way. Today, literacy is much more focused on finding and vetting relevant information from a wide variety of viewpoints, making sense of it, and being able to communicate original ideas that are based on this information to a global audience. Studies show that when students use technology to analyze information and make predictions, they increase cognitive load and understanding (Li & Liu, 2007).

If students only have opportunities to demonstrate their ability to remember, understand, or apply what they learn in school, they are ill-prepared for higher-level thinking outside the classroom. After all, it is a rare instance in life when we are simply presented with questions to which there is only one correct answer. Asking students to generate and test hypotheses moves them beyond "right-answer learning," gives them opportunities to learn how to learn, and tests current beliefs and understandings. In this way, we give students the ultimate gift of education: the ability to educate oneself and use that knowledge in productive ways.

## Tips for Teaching Using Generating and Testing Hypotheses

1. Provide minilessons to help students better understand the individual steps of each type of task, how to develop a good hypothesis, or how to write a good explanation of their conclusions.
2. When asking students to use an inductive approach to generating and testing hypotheses, design a set of learning experiences that provide sufficient and suitable opportunities for students to infer accurate and appropriate principles from which to generate hypotheses. Check student understanding with formative assessment to ensure that the learning experiences did not reinforce misconceptions.
3. To increase motivation and interest, involve students in designing their own tasks and contributing to the development of rubrics for explaining their hypotheses and conclusions. Provide students with choices about how they are grouped, which type of task they complete, and how they explain their results.
4. Teach the underlying structures for each of the cognitive processes (i.e., systems analysis, problem solving, experimental inquiry, investigation) to help students carry out the steps of the processes and recognize which situations are best suited to each.

# Part IV

## Putting the Instructional Strategies to Use

# 10

# Instructional Planning Using the Nine Categories of Strategies

"Simply using the strategies at random will not raise student achievement; teachers must also understand how, when, and why to use them."

—Bryan Goodwin, *Simply Better*

The instructional strategies presented in the previous chapters are like instruments in an orchestra. Each has its own characteristics, contributes to the orchestra in particular ways, and must be masterfully played both alone and in combination with other instruments to obtain the desired effect. The orchestra's conductor must know when to emphasize each of the instruments and how to bring out their particular qualities in order to accomplish the purpose of the music. An orchestra sounds best when the composer selects the most appropriate instruments and the conductor blends those instruments in just the right way to create the desired sound. To be skilled conductors of instruction, teachers must intentionally select the best mix of instructional strategies to meet the diverse needs of students in their classrooms. This chapter helps teachers accomplish that goal by providing guidance that addresses the components of the instructional planning framework and the use of the nine categories of strategies for teaching different types of knowledge.

## Instructional Planning: Creating the Environment for Learning

Instructional planning begins with focused attention on creating a productive environment for learning. The three categories of strategies included in this component of the framework include

- Setting Objectives and Providing Feedback
- Reinforcing Effort and Providing Recognition
- Cooperative Learning

These strategies are foundational because they involve the articulation of what students will learn, how their learning will be evaluated, and how closely they pay attention to the affective aspects of learning. When teachers do not attend to the latter, student motivation often suffers, causing students to miss out on opportunities to acquire a range of skills that help them be lifelong learners and productive workers and citizens. The following sections provide guidance to help teachers lay a strong foundation for instruction.

### Identify learning objectives

The first question teachers should ask themselves is "What should students know, understand, and be able to do by the end of this unit or lesson?" The answer to this basic question will be found by conducting a thorough investigation of the content and skills located in your district- or school-adopted standards and curriculum documents. Using these documents as the starting point for planning ensures that students have opportunities to learn the required knowledge. Once you've identified appropriate learning objectives, you can think about which students have the prerequisite knowledge and skills, which activities help students acquire the relevant knowledge and skills, and how you might group students to address their various learning needs. The following checklist is meant to help teachers effectively set objectives in their classrooms:

1. Tightly align learning objectives with the guidance provided in the Common Core State Standards or in district or state standards and curriculum documents.

2. Ensure learning objectives are
   - Written in student-friendly language that clearly reflects the content or skills that students are expected to learn.
   - Written in terms of the knowledge and skills to be learned rather than of the activities in which students will be engaged.
3. Include opportunities to determine students' existing knowledge and skills in addition to misconceptions related to the objectives.
4. Clearly align all of the learning experiences in the unit/lesson with the objectives.
5. Reference the learning objectives throughout the unit/lesson.
6. Provide opportunities for students to connect what they are learning and doing to the objectives of the unit/lesson.
7. Articulate connections between the objectives of the unit/lesson and those of previous units so it is clear how these objectives fit in the overall course.

## Identify criteria for evaluating student performance

Teachers should give considerable thought to performance criteria as they plan units/lessons; they must have checkpoints to determine whether the learning experiences they design for students are ones that will help them achieve proficiency. Identifying the criteria for performance helps teachers think about when and how they might assess student learning and provide formal feedback. Sharing clearly defined criteria with students helps them better understand the relevant learning objectives and what they must know or do to meet expectations.

District curriculum documents may include guidance on student performance criteria by including rubrics for evaluating various components of student work. If guidance is not available in district documents, teachers can find examples of rubrics for a variety of topics online, including state-sponsored assessment websites. Such rubrics might require some modification to fit particular circumstances, so teachers should be sure to examine them closely for alignment with what their students need to know, understand, and be able to do.

We have emphasized that feedback is a carefully crafted set of information that teachers provide to help students shape their understanding of content or develop skills and processes. A checklist to guide instructional planning with regard to evaluating student performance and providing feedback follows:

1. Clearly define criteria against which student performance will be judged.
2. Tightly align performance criteria with the learning objectives.
3. Decide when and how performance criteria will be shared with students.
4. Identify specific times and ways to formatively assess student performance with regard to the learning objectives.
5. Designate specific times when students will receive formal feedback on their progress toward proficiency.
6. Decide how and when students will provide their own feedback.

## Attend to effort and metacognition

If students do not see the relevance of the learning objectives or believe they can successfully achieve them, it is unlikely they will fully engage in the learning activities their teachers identify. When teachers reinforce effort, provide recognition for accomplishments, and involve students in cooperative learning, they can positively influence how students think about their ability to succeed. Teachers can help students recognize the control they have over their own learning and how this affects whether the teacher and other students accept them as a member of the classroom community. That's why it is important to consider the following strategies when planning for instruction.

### Reinforcing Effort

Helping students develop the belief that the harder they work, the smarter they will get empowers them to "own" their learning and take pride in their academic accomplishments (Dweck, 2006). When teachers help students develop a growth-oriented mind-set, students are more likely to persist in the face of challenges. The following checklist can guide teachers' approaches to reinforcing effort in instructional planning:

1. Identify optimal times to address the relationship between effort and achievement in the unit/lesson.

2. Define in student-friendly language what it means to put forth effort in the class for the unit/lesson and determine when and how to share this information with students.

3. Identify stories or examples relevant to the unit/lesson that illustrate the relationship between effort and achievement.

4. Determine when to provide opportunities for students to share their own stories about effort and success.

5. Provide ongoing opportunities for students to track their effort and relate their success to their effort.

### Providing Recognition

Providing recognition for accomplishments underscores the value of working toward a goal that is worth achieving. It also encourages people to keep trying, even in the face of challenges. As teachers plan for instruction, they should think about the most important times to provide recognition and the best ways to do so. They also should identify students who might struggle to succeed in a unit/lesson and require more encouragement, or encouragement in a different form, than other students need. The following checklist provides guidance for providing recognition in instructional planning:

1. Identify specific achievements in the unit/lesson that will be recognized.

2. Determine points in the unit/lesson when it is most important to provide recognition for progress toward the identified achievements.

3. Identify students for whom it is most important to provide recognition during the unit/lesson.

4. Determine when to provide opportunities for students to recognize one another's accomplishments.

5. Determine what forms of recognition you will provide, paying particular attention to how students' personalities, ages, and cultures might influence their preferences for how recognition is provided.

6. If tangible tokens of recognition will be used in the unit/lesson, decide what form they will take.

**Cooperative Learning**

As we saw in Chapter 3, participating in cooperative learning helps students develop a number of skills, including academically based social skills that will serve them in school and the workplace. To ensure effective use of cooperative learning, teachers need to think about when it is best to ask students to work independently and when to ask them to work in groups during the unit/lesson. They also need to think about when and how to use formal and informal cooperative learning groups and the balance of large-group instruction and cooperative groups. Keeping in mind the following points will help teachers make these decisions (Frey, Fisher, & Everlove, 2009):

- Use cooperative learning to
  - help students clarify, consolidate, and expand their understanding of the content by using and building on the ideas of peers.
  - encourage the exchange of ideas among students.
- Use cooperative learning when students are ready to tackle a challenge or solve a problem. If the cooperative learning experience occurs before students are ready, they may become frustrated and give up. Students are ready when they
  - know the purpose of the learning.
  - have been provided with a model for completing the task.
  - have had sufficient guided practice in using the skills required for the task.
- Use cooperative learning to provide opportunities for students to wrestle with ideas, create meaning, and work independently of (but with guidance from) the teacher.
- Use cooperative learning techniques systematically (at least once a week).
- Use cooperative learning in different types of groups (e.g., informal, formal, or base) that are designed for different purposes.
- Use cooperative learning techniques that include positive interdependence as well as individual and group accountability.
- Do not overuse cooperative learning; students need sufficient time to practice independently the skills and processes they must master.

Depending on students' various levels of experience and expertise working in cooperative learning groups, teachers might have to include time for teaching or reviewing group skills in their unit/lesson plans. A checklist to guide instructional planning related to cooperative learning follows:

1. Consider whether students need to learn or review group skills. If so, plan to include a lesson on protocols for participating in cooperative groups before expecting students to use group skills to accomplish content-related tasks.

2. Determine which classroom activities require students to work in cooperative groups.

3. For each of the identified activities, determine whether groups will be formal or informal, what roles students will fulfill, and how students will be held accountable individually and as groups.

4. Find or create checklists or rubrics to provide feedback to students on how well they accomplish the task, fulfill their individual roles, and function as a group.

5. Include opportunities for students to process and learn from their cooperative learning experiences during the unit/lesson.

6. Check the balance between large groups and cooperative groups to determine if it is appropriate for what students need to learn and the amount of independent practice they need in order to learn it.

## Instructional Planning: Helping Students Develop Understanding

The strategies discussed in the previous section laid the foundation for instruction. Now it is time to consider which strategies will help students achieve learning objectives as new content is introduced. The general question "What strategies should I use to help students connect to and build on prior learning?" is addressed with the following strategies:

- Cues, Questions, and Advance Organizers
- Nonlinguistic Representations
- Summarizing and Note Taking
- Assigning Homework and Providing Practice

In this section, we discuss how to use these strategies in combination with Setting Objectives and Providing Feedback to teach specific types of knowledge as students develop their understanding of new knowledge and integrate it with what they already know.

## Teach two types of knowledge

You might be wondering what we mean by "specific types of knowledge" and why it is important to make distinctions among them. Here, we discuss two types of knowledge that are emphasized in schools: declarative knowledge and procedural knowledge. Declarative knowledge is informational in nature and includes vocabulary terms and phrases, details (e.g., facts, dates, time sequences), and organizing ideas (generalizations and principles). Procedural knowledge is process oriented and includes skills, tactics, and processes. Figure 10.1 illustrates the five broad categories of subject-matter knowledge and how they are organized from specific to general. Learning objectives for declarative knowledge ask students to know vocabulary and details and understand generalizations and principles. Learning objectives for procedural knowledge ask students to perform skills, tactics, and processes. We pay attention to different types of knowledge because there is evidence that different types of knowledge require different types of teaching (Madaus & Stufflebeam, 1989; Taba, 1962).

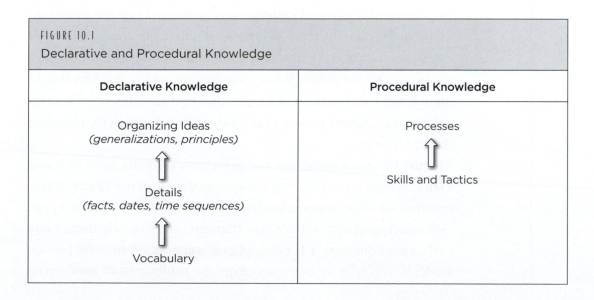

FIGURE 10.1
Declarative and Procedural Knowledge

| Declarative Knowledge | Procedural Knowledge |
|---|---|
| Organizing Ideas *(generalizations, principles)* ⬆ Details *(facts, dates, time sequences)* ⬆ Vocabulary | Processes ⬆ Skills and Tactics |

### Plan for initial learning of declarative knowledge

Declarative knowledge can be arranged in a hierarchy that includes vocabulary terms and phrases, which are very specific in nature, at one end and generalizations and principles, which are very general in nature, at the other end. The following list provides guidance for instructional planning when helping students develop an understanding of new declarative knowledge and how to integrate it with what they already know.

1. **Identify the words and phrases that are most important to the content that students are learning.** Determine which of the words will be taught directly and when they will be taught using a systematic process that includes first the teacher and then students creating a nonlinguistic representation for each word. This practice is especially important for English language learners because it allows them to develop meaning for words as they learn English.

2. **Identify the details students need to learn.** To help students learn these details, plan learning experiences that include use of cues, questions, and advance organizers to activate students' prior knowledge and prepare them to make connections between what they already know and what they are about to learn. In addition, use structured note taking, graphic organizers, and dramatic presentations to help students focus on important details and understand how those details are connected to one another, to the topic as a whole, and to major concepts in other units/lessons. Consider whether you should include opportunities for students to act out details. When planning instruction, teachers should identify the specific cues, questions, advance organizers, graphic organizers, and dramatic presentations they will use to teach the details in the unit/lesson.

3. **Identify the generalizations and principles students need to learn.** Plan learning experiences that incorporate the use of nonlinguistic representations when students first learn generalizations or principles (e.g., "We understand that animals have characteristics that help them adapt to their environments"). For example, use a graphic organizer to provide students with relevant examples or involve students in an appropriate

dramatization of the generalization or principle. Using metaphors and analogies to provide students with a mental framework can help them grasp the generalizations and principles that are particularly difficult to understand. When planning for instruction, teachers need to find or create the graphic organizers, dramatic presentation suggestions, metaphors, and analogies that will be used to teach the generalizations and principles in the unit/lesson.

4. **Determine how to provide feedback to students about declarative knowledge in the unit/lesson.** Feedback on declarative knowledge when students are developing an initial understanding should focus on such dimensions as accuracy of facts, level and completeness of detail, and appropriate examples of the generalizations and principles.

5. **Identify homework assignments that help students deepen their understanding of declarative knowledge in the unit/lesson or help them make additional connections.** Homework assignments should include opportunities to use the vocabulary of the unit/lesson, connect facts and details to other units/lessons, or find examples of the generalizations or principles.

## Plan for initial learning of procedural knowledge

Learning procedural knowledge occurs in three phases: constructing models, shaping, and internalizing (Figure 10.2). Procedural knowledge includes skills and processes such as following steps in a recipe or formula, solving multistep problems, summarizing information found in texts, and using prewriting strategies to plan written work.

The following list provides guidance for instructional planning when helping students develop an understanding of new procedural knowledge and integrate it with what they already know.

1. Review the learning objectives to determine which skills students need to learn during the unit/lesson and whether those skills need to be taught directly. To introduce a skill that must be executed in a specific order, plan to teach the skill directly and demonstrate it for students. The demonstration might include cues, questions, advance organizers,

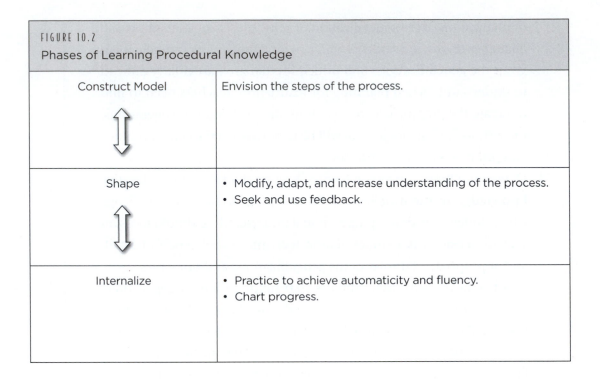

FIGURE 10.2

Phases of Learning Procedural Knowledge

| Construct Model | Envision the steps of the process. |
| --- | --- |
| Shape | • Modify, adapt, and increase understanding of the process.<br>• Seek and use feedback. |
| Internalize | • Practice to achieve automaticity and fluency.<br>• Chart progress. |

or nonlinguistic representations. When the steps of a skill can be executed in a number of ways, provide opportunities for students to engage in inquiry learning to examine those different approaches. Planning should include the creation of examples that are categorized according to different approaches to the skill. For example, in mathematics, several variations on subtraction problems are possible:

- *Result unknown:* 8 − 3 = ?
- *Change unknown:* 8 − ? = 5
- *Start unknown:* ? − 3 = 5

Each of these variations presents specific challenges for students as they learn what subtraction means and how to perform the operation of subtraction. Students can then design strategies for each category and compare their strategies to develop an understanding of the skill and how to perform it. As teachers plan instruction, they can include opportunities for students to take notes and summarize what they are learning about the skill and how it connects to their prior knowledge and to larger processes.

2. Identify the processes students need to learn during the unit/lesson. Plan how to provide students with links to their prior knowledge during the initial phase of instruction—the "construct a model of the process" phase—by using cues, questions, and advance organizers or nonlinguistic representations. Then use note taking, summarizing, and nonlinguistic representations to provide students with some information about the general aspects of the processes, a general model of the overall components and subcomponents of the processes, and opportunities to make connections between the processes and the content of the unit/lesson.

3. Determine how and when to provide opportunities for students to practice. When teachers help students initially acquire a skill or process, they should include opportunities for frequent (massed) practice with feedback. Instructional planning for procedural knowledge should include sufficient opportunities for students to engage in guided practice with feedback prior to moving them to independent practice.

4. Determine how to provide feedback to students on the procedural knowledge in the unit/lesson. Feedback on procedural knowledge should focus on such dimensions as accuracy and speed.

5. Identify practice and homework assignments that help students use the skill or process effectively and efficiently. Practice sessions and homework assignments should include opportunities for students to independently practice the skill or process to increase accuracy and speed.

## Instructional Planning: Helping Students Extend and Apply Knowledge

As the unit/lesson unfolds, the goal moves from introducing new knowledge to helping students extend that knowledge and apply their learning to new situations. In this section, we revisit and provide supplementary information about the specific strategies for helping students extend and apply their learning:

- Identifying Similarities and Differences
- Generating and Testing Hypotheses

## Plan for extending and applying learning of declarative knowledge

Teachers can provide opportunities for students to extend and apply their learning of declarative knowledge by using strategies that require students to think deeply about the relationships among ideas. This means unit/lesson plans should include opportunities for students to engage in learning activities that involve identifying similarities and differences and generating and testing hypotheses. For example, as students deepen their understanding of vocabulary words and phrases, they might participate in activities that require them to classify and categorize words or make connections among them. They might develop analogies that emphasize the relationships between pairs of words or metaphors that apply the meaning of the word to a different context. Similarly, teachers can include opportunities for students to act out the details of a particular event, generate and represent examples of generalizations or principles, or apply generalizations and principles to new situations.

The following list guides instructional planning for helping students extend and apply declarative knowledge:

1. Plan opportunities for students to make connections among new vocabulary by making comparisons, classifying, or creating metaphors or analogies that involve the words or phrases.

2. Plan opportunities for students to read metaphors or analogies that the teacher finds or creates—or that students create on their own—to help them deepen their understanding of the generalizations and principles in the unit/lesson.

3. Determine whether students need minilessons on the processes of systems analysis, problem solving, experimental inquiry, and investigation; on how to develop a good hypothesis; or on how to write a good explanation of conclusions before they are asked to engage in generating and testing hypotheses.

4. Find or create tasks that require students to generate and test hypotheses about the details, generalizations, and principles of a unit/lesson as they engage in the processes of systems analysis, problem solving, experimental inquiry, or investigation.

5. Plan in-class and homework assignments that require students to generate examples of generalizations and principles or apply them to new situations.

6. Provide feedback that focuses on the application of generalizations and principles to new situations.

## Plan for extending and applying learning of procedural knowledge

To help students extend and apply learning of procedural knowledge, teachers should include opportunities for students to develop automaticity of skills and processes. This can be achieved by planning for distributed practice over time (i.e., during and after the lesson/unit). Figure 10.3 illustrates how teachers might track their plans for providing students with distributed practice across topics within a content area for a whole year. Teachers can add to the chart as they plan for each lesson/unit.

Processes involve complex interactions among component skills. Learning a process involves mastering the component skills as well as consciously controlling the interactions among the skills. This is referred to as metacognitive control, which includes strategies for

- Establishing a personalized specific goal for engaging in the process.
- Activating specific component skills or processes to accomplish the goal.
- Monitoring the timing and use of component skills and processes.
- Monitoring dispositions (e.g., accuracy and precision, clarity, restraint of impulsivity, intensity of task engagement and focus). (Marzano, 1998)

Engaging in activities that focus on controlling the metacognitive aspects of learning a process helps students develop automaticity of skills and processes. Planning should address how to provide students with feedback that improves the execution of metacognitive strategies and provides opportunities to apply them to different tasks in different content areas.

The following list guides instructional planning for helping students extend and apply procedural knowledge:

1. Plan for distributed practice of skills and processes during and after the unit/lesson.

FIGURE 10.3
Tracking Distributed Practice by Topic over Time

| Skills | Aug | Sept | Oct | Nov | Dec | Jan | Feb | March | April |
|---|---|---|---|---|---|---|---|---|---|
| Using a microscope | Originally taught with three practices during unit on classroom science equipment | Two practices with feedback during unit on plant and animal cells | | Three practices with feedback during unit on photosynthesis | Two practices with feedback during unit on circulation within cells | | Four practices with feedback during unit on digestion and respiration in single-celled organisms | Four practices with feedback during unit on yeasts and bacteria | Five practices with feedback during unit on pond water |
| Creating a wet-mount slide | | Originally taught with five practices and feedback during unit on plant and animal cells | | Three practices with feedback during unit on photosynthesis | | | | | Five practices with feedback during unit on pond water |
| Using a Bunsen burner | Originally taught with three practices and feedback during unit on classroom science equipment and safety | | Four practices with feedback (flame tests) | | | Eight practices with feedback during unit on proteins, carbohydrates | Four practices with feedback during unit on digestion (inactivating enzymes) | Four practices with feedback during unit on yeasts and bacteria (sterilize inoculation loop) | |

2. Provide feedback that focuses on the automaticity of students' use of skills and processes and their understanding of the key features of the skills and processes.

3. Provide opportunities for students to focus on the metacognitive aspects of learning a process, and provide feedback on how well they execute metacognitive strategies.

4. Provide homework assignments that focus on developing automaticity of the skills and processes in the unit/lesson.

Figure 10.4 summarizes information about the key instructional practices for teaching each type of knowledge and identifies which of the instructional strategies are most useful for helping students acquire, extend, and apply that knowledge.

## Moving from Knowing to Doing

Instructional planning requires careful thought when the goal is to help all students succeed. The information in this book can help teachers frame their thinking about instructional planning and move them from *knowing* about research-based instructional strategies to *doing* what's most appropriate with those strategies. With this systematic approach to planning, teachers demonstrate their commitment to teaching and optimize the opportunities they provide for student learning.

FIGURE 10.4
Key Instructional Practice for Teaching Types of Knowledge

| Type of Knowledge | Key Instructional Practices | Strategies That Support Teaching |
|---|---|---|
| Vocabulary | • Identify the words and phrases that are critical to learning new content.<br>• Use an instructional sequence that allows for multiple exposures to new words or phrases in multiple ways.<br>  – Provide students with a brief explanation or description and nonlinguistic representation of the word.<br>  – Ask students to generate their own explanation and nonlinguistic representation of the word.<br>  – Ask students to review their definitions periodically to check for accuracy.<br>• Engage students in vocabulary games. | • Setting Objectives<br>• Nonlinguistic Representation<br>• Identifying Similarities and Differences |
| Details *(facts, dates, time sequences)* | • Identify the important details students should learn.<br>• Tell the class about details or have students read about them.<br>• Provide students with a dramatic representation of important details. | • Setting Objectives<br>• Cues, Questions, and Advance Organizers<br>• Nonlinguistic Representation<br>• Summarizing and Note Taking<br>• Identifying Similarities and Differences |

FIGURE 10.4
Key Instructional Practice for Teaching Types of Knowledge (continued)

| Type of Knowledge | Key Instructional Practices | Strategies That Support Teaching |
|---|---|---|
| Organizing Ideas (generalizations, principles) | • Ask students to discuss what they know about a generalization or principle.<br>• Ask students to provide a sound argument or defense for a position or provide them with one.<br>• Once students have an initial grasp of generalizations and principles, ask them to apply them to a variety of situations.<br>• Ask students to clearly articulate statements of generalizations and principles.<br>• Ask students to generate numerous examples of the targeted generalizations and principles. | • Cooperative Learning<br>• Nonlinguistic Representation<br>• Generating and Testing Hypotheses |
| Skills | • Directly teach skills that involve specific steps that need to be executed in a specific order.<br>• Demonstrate the skill.<br>• Provide opportunities for students to learn skills to the level of automaticity.<br>• When using the inquiry approach to teaching a skill, provide students with examples organized in categories.<br>• Ask students to design strategies for each category and then to compare the strategies developed for the different categories.<br>• Use simulations to provide opportunities for students to identify strategies for executing and practicing the skill.<br>• Plan for massed practice early in the learning cycle and distributed practice over time (e.g., several months). | • Nonlinguistic Representation<br>• Identifying Similarities and Differences<br>• Cooperative Learning<br>• Generating and Testing Hypotheses<br>• Providing Practice |

continued

FIGURE 10.4
Key Instructional Practice for Teaching Types of Knowledge

| Type of Knowledge | Key Instructional Practices | Strategies That Support Teaching |
|---|---|---|
| Processes | • Provide students with some guidance in the general aspects of the process.<br>• Provide students with a general model of the overall components and subcomponents of the process.<br>• Provide opportunities for students to practice parts of the process in the context of the overall process, and clearly articulate the aspect of the process that is the focus of learning.<br>   – Provide focused practice.<br>   – Present the components and subcomponents of the process.<br>   – Structure tasks to emphasize a specific component or subcomponent within the complete process.<br>   – Provide feedback on the specific component or subcomponent.<br>• Emphasize the metacognitive aspects of learning a process (i.e., understanding and controlling the interactions among the component parts of the process at a conscious level).<br>   – Provide plenty of guided practice with feedback on how to improve execution of the metacognitive strategies (e.g., goal specification, process specification, monitoring process, monitoring disposition).<br>   – Encourage students to monitor their performance when using the metacognitive strategies.<br>   – Encourage generalization of the metacognitive strategies by having students use them with different materials in different content areas. | • Setting Objectives<br>• Nonlinguistic Representation<br>• Providing Practice<br>• Providing Feedback |

# References

Alderman, M. K. (2008). *Motivation for achievement.* (3rd ed.). New York: Routledge.

Anderson, J. R. (1995). *Learning and memory: An integrated approach.* New York: Wiley.

Anderson, J. R., Reder, L. M., & Simon, H. A. (1997). *Applications and misapplications of cognitive psychology to mathematics education.* Unpublished manuscript, Carnegie Mellon University, Pittsburgh, PA.

Anderson, T. H., & Armbruster, B. B. (1986). *The value of taking notes during lectures.* (Tech. Rep. No. 374). Cambridge, MA: Bolt, Beranek & Newman; and Urbana, IL: Center for the Study of Reading. (ERIC Document Reproduction Service No. ED 277 996)

Anderson, V., & Hidi, S. (1988/1989). Teaching students to summarize. *Educational Leadership, 46,* 26–28.

Anderson, W. L. (2005). Comparison of student performance in cooperative learning and traditional lecture-based biochemistry classes. *Biochemistry and Molecular Biology Education, 33*(6), 387–393.

Antil, L. R., Jenkins, J. R., Wayne, S. K., & Vadasy, P. F. (1998). CL: Prevalence, conceptualizations, and the relation between research and practice. *American Educational Research Journal, 35,* 419–454.

Aronson, E., Stephan, C., Stikes, J., Blaney, N., & Snapp, M. (1978). *The jigsaw classroom.* Beverly Hills, CA: Sage.

Ausubel, D. P. (1960). The use of advance organizers in the learning and retention of meaningful verbal material. *Journal of Educational Psychology, 51,* 267–272.

Bailey, L. B., Silvern, S. B., Brabham, E., & Ross, M. (2004). The effects of interactive reading homework and parent involvement on children's inference responses. *Early Childhood Education Journal, 32*(3), 173–178.

Balli, S. J. (1998). When mom and dad help: Student reflections on parent involvement with homework. *Journal of Research and Development in Education, 31*(3), 142–148.

Balli, S. J., Demo, D. H., & Wedman, J. F. (1998). Family involvement with children's homework: An intervention in the middle grades. *Family Relations: Interdisciplinary Journal of Applied Family Studies, 47*(2), 149–157.

Bandura, A. (1986). *Social foundations of thought and action: A social cognitive theory.* Englewood Cliffs, NJ: Prentice-Hall.

Bandura, A. (2000). Exercise of human agency through collective efficacy. *Current Directions in Psychological Science, 9*(3), 75–78.

Barber, M., & Mourshed, M. (2007, September). *How the world's best-performing school systems come out on top*. New York: McKinsey & Company.

Baser, M., & Geban, Ö. (2007). Effectiveness of conceptual change instruction on understanding of heat and temperature concepts. *Research in Science & Technology Education, 25*(1), 115–133.

Beesley, A. D., & Apthorp, H. S. (Eds.). (2010). *Classroom instruction that works, second edition: Research report*. Denver, CO: Mid-continent Research for Education and Learning.

Blank, M., Rose, S. A., & Berlin, L. J. (2003). *Preschool Language Assessment Instrument: The language of learning in practice* (2nd ed.). Austin, TX: PRO-ED.

Block, C. C., Gambrell, L. B., & Pressley, M. (Eds.). (2002). *Improving comprehension instruction: Rethinking research, theory, and classroom practice*. San Francisco: Wiley.

Boch, F., & Piolat, A. (2005). Note taking and learning: A Summary of research. *The WAC Journal, 16*, 101–113.

Bos, B. (2007). The effect of the Texas Instrument interactive instructional environment on the mathematical achievement of eleventh grade low achieving students. *Journal of Educational Computing Research, 37*(4), 351–368.

Bottge, B., Rueda, E., & Skivington, M. (2006). Situating math instruction in rich problem-solving contexts: Effects on adolescents with challenging behaviors. *Behavioral Disorders, 31*, 394–407.

Bouffard, T., Boisvert, J., Vezeau, C., & Larouche, C. (1995). The impact of goal orientation on self-regulation and performance among college students. *British Journal of Educational Psychology, 65*(3), 317–330.

BouJaoude, S., & Tamin, R. (1998). *Analogies, summaries, and question answering in middle school life science: Effect on achievement and perceptions of instructional value*. Paper presented at the annual meeting of the National Association for Research in Science Teaching, April 19–22, San Diego, CA. (ERIC Document Reproduction Service No. ED 420 503)

Bransford, J., Brown, A., & Cocking, R. (1999). *How people learn: Brain, mind, experience, and school*. Washington, DC: National Academies Press.

Bransford, J., Brown, A., & Cocking, R. (2000). *How people learn: Brain, mind, experience, and school* (Expanded ed.). Washington, DC: National Academies Press.

Broer, N., Aarnoutse, C., Kieviet, F., & van Leeuwe, J. (2002). The effects of instructing the structural aspects of text. *Educational Studies, (28)*3, 213–238.

Brookhart, S. M. (2008). *How to give effective feedback*. Alexandria, VA: ASCD.

Brophy, J. (2004). *Motivating students to learn* (2nd ed.). Boston, MA: McGraw-Hill.

Brophy, J., & Good, T. (1986). Teacher behavior and student achievement. In M. Wittrock (Ed.), *Handbook of research on teaching* (pp. 328–375). New York: Macmillan.

Caram, C., & Davis, P. (2005). Inviting student engagement with questioning. *Kappa Delta Pi Record, 41*(3), 18–23.

Carpenter, S. K., Pashler, H., & Cepeda, J. (2009). Using tests to enhance 8th grade students' retention of U.S. history facts. *Applied Cognitive Psychology, 23*, 760–771.

Cepeda, N. J., Pashler, H., Vul, E., Wixted, J. T., & Rohrer, D. (2006). Distributed practice in verbal recall tasks: A review and qualitative synthesis. *Psychological Bulletin, 132*(3), 354–380.

Chen, Z. (1999). Schema induction in children's analogical problem solving. *Journal of Educational Psychology, 91*(4), 703–715.

Cialdini, R. B. (2005). What's the best secret device for engaging student interest? Hint: The answer's in the title. *Journal of Social and Clinical Psychology, 24*(1), 22–29.

Clariana, R. B., & Koul, R. (2006). The effects of different forms of feedback on fuzzy and verbatim memory of science principles. *British Journal of Educational Psychology, 76*, 259–270.

Clark, J., & Paivio, A. (1991). Dual coding theory and education. *Educational Psychology Review, 3*, 149–210.

Clement, J., Lockhead, J., & Mink, G. (1979). Translation difficulties in learning mathematics. *American Mathematical Monthly, 88*, 3–7.

Cohen, E. (1994). *Designing group work: Strategies for the heterogeneous classroom*. New York: Teachers College Press.

Conley, D. T. (2007). *Redefining college readiness* (Vol. 3). Eugene, OR: Educational Policy Improvement Center.

Cooper, H. M. (1989). Synthesis of research on homework. *Educational Leadership, 47*(3), 85–91.

Cooper, H. M. (2007). *The battle over homework: Common ground for administrators, teachers, and parents* (3rd ed.). Thousand Oaks, CA: Corwin.

Cooper, H., Lindsay, J. J., Nye, B., & Greathouse, S. (1998). Relationships among attitudes about homework, amount of homework assigned and completed, and student achievement. *Journal of Educational Psychology, 90*(1), 70–83.

Cooper, H., Robinson, J. C., & Patall, E.A. (2006). Does homework improve academic achievement?: A synthesis of research, 1987–2003. *Review of Educational Research, 76*(1), 1–62.

Coutts, P. (2004). Meanings of homework and implications for practice. *Theory into Practice 43*(3), 182–188.

Covington, M. V. (1992). *Making the grade: A self-worth perspective on motivation and school reform*. New York: Cambridge University Press.

Darling-Hammond, L., Barron, B., Pearson, P. D., Schoenfeld, A. H., Stage, E. K., Zimmerman, T. D., Cervetti, G. N., & Tilson, J. L. (2008). *Powerful learning: What we know about teaching for understanding*. San Francisco: Wiley.

Davis, R. B. (1984). *Learning mathematics: The cognitive science approach to mathematics education*. Norwood, NJ: Ablex.

Deci, E. L., & Ryan, R. M. (1985). *Intrinsic motivation and self determination in human behavior*. New York: Plenum.

Denner, P. R. (1986). *Comparison of the effects of episodic organizers and traditional notetaking on story recall* (Final Report). Boise: Idaho State University. (ERIC Document Reproduction Service No. ED 270 731)

DeVries, D. L., & Edwards, K. J. (1973). Learning Games and Student Teams: Their effects on classroom process. *American Educational Research Journal, 10*(4), 307–318.

Diperna, J. C. (2006). Academic enablers and student achievement: Implications for assessment and intervention services in the schools. *Psychology in the Schools, 43*(1), 7–17.

Donovan, J., & Radosevich, D. (1999). A meta-analytic review of the distribution of practice effect: Now you see it, now you don't. *Journal of Applied Psychology, 84*(5), 795–805.

Donovan, S., & Bransford, J. D. (2005). *How students learn: History, mathematics, and science in the classroom*. Washington DC: National Academies Press.

Dweck, C. (2006). *Mindset: The new psychology of success*. New York: Random House.

Earley, P. C. (1989). Social loafing and collectivism: A comparison of the United States and the People's Republic of China. *Administrative Science Quarterly, 34*(4), 565–581.

Eccles, J.S., Wigfield, A., & Schiefele, U. (1998). Motivation to succeed. In N. Eisenberg (Ed.), *Handbook of child psychology: Volume 3—Social, emotional, and personality development* (5th ed. pp. 1017–1096). New York: Wiley.

Einstein, G. O., Morris, J., & Smith, S. (1985). Notetaking, individual differences, and memory for lecture information. *Journal of Educational Psychology, 77*(5), 522–532.

Elliot, E. S., McGregor, H. A., & Gable, S. L. (1999). Achievement goals, study strategies, and exam performance: A mediational analysis. *Journal of Educational Psychology, 91*, 549–563.

Fillippone, M. (1998). *Questioning at the elementary level*. Master's thesis, Kean University. (ERIC Document Reproduction Service No. ED 417 421)

Fisch, K., & McLeod, S. (2007). *Did you know? (Shift happens.)* [Videotape]. Retrieved from http://www.youtube.com/watch?v=pMcfrLYDm2U

Franzke, M., Kintsch, E., Caccamise, D., Johnson, N., & Dooley, S. (2005). Summary Street®: Computer support for comprehension and writing. *Journal of Educational Computing Research, 33*(1), 53–80.

Frayer, D., Frederick, W. C., & Klausmeier, H. J. (1969). *A schema for testing the level of cognitive mastery*. Madison, WI: Wisconsin Center for Education Research.

Frey, N., Fisher, D., & Everlove, S. (2009). *Productive group work: How to engage students, build teamwork, and promote understanding*. Alexandria, VA: ASCD.

Frey, N., Fisher, D., & Gonzalez, A. (2010). *Literacy 2.0: Reading and writing in the 21st century classrooms*. Bloomington, IN: Solution Tree.

Friedman, T. (2006). *The world is flat: A brief history of the twenty-first century* (2nd ed.). New York: Farrar, Straus and Giroux.

Fuchs, L. S., Fuchs, D., Finelli, R., Courey, S. J., Hamlett, C. L., Sones, E. M., & Hope, S. (2006). Teaching third graders about real-life mathematical problem solving: A randomized controlled study. *Elementary School Journal, 106*, 293–312.

Garner, B. (2007). *Getting to "got it!" Helping struggling students learn how to learn*. Alexandria, VA: ASCD.

Garofano, A., & Sable, J. (2008). *Characteristics of the 100 largest public elementary and secondary school districts in the United States: 2005–06* (NCES 2008-339). National Center for Education Statistics, Institute of Education Sciences, U.S. Department of Education. Washington, DC.

Gentner, D., Loewenstein, J., & Thompson, L. (2003). Learning and transfer: A general role for analogical encoding. *Journal of Educational Psychology, 95*, 393–408.

Gerlach, J. M. (1994). Is this collaboration? In K. Bosworth and S. J. Hamilton (Eds.), *Collaborative learning: Underlying processes and effective techniques, new directions for teaching and learning* (p. 59). San Francisco: Jossey-Bass.

Gill B. P., & Schlossman, S. L. (2003). A nation at rest: The American way of homework. *Educational Evaluation and Policy Analysis, 25*(3), 319–337.

Glaser, C., & Brunstein, J. C. (2007). Improving fourth-grade students' composition skills: Effects of strategy instruction and self-regulation procedures. *Journal of Educational Psychology 99*, 297–310.

Goodwin, B. (2010). *Changing the odds for student success: What matters most*. Retrieved from www.changtheodds.org

Goodwin, B. (2011). *Simply better: Doing what matters most to change the odds for student success*. Alexandria, VA: ASCD.

Goodwin, B., Lefkowits, L., Woempner, C., & Hubbell, E. (2011). *The future of schooling: Educating America in 2020*. Bloomington, IN: Solution Tree.

Greene, B. A., Miller, R. B., Crowson, H. M., Duke, B. L., & Akey, K. L. (2004). Predicting high school students' cognitive engagement and achievement: Contributions of classroom perceptions and motivation. *Contemporary Educational Psychology, 29*(4), 462–482.

Greenwood, S.E. (2002). Contracting revisited: Lessons learned in literacy differentiation. *Journal of Adolescent and Adult Literacy, 46*, 338–349.

Guerin, B. (1999). Social behaviors as determined by different arrangements of social consequences: Social loafing, social facilitation, deindividuation, and a modified social loafing. *The Psychological Record, 49*, 565–578.

Hall, K. G., Domingues, D. A., & Cavazos, R. (1994). Contextual interference effects with skilled baseball players. *Perceptual and Motor Skills, 78*, 835–841.

Hamilton, S. L., Seibert, M. A., Gardner, R., III, & Talbert-Johnson, C. (2000). Using guided notes to improve the academic achievement of incarcerated adolescents with learning and behavior problems. *Remedial & Special Education, 21*(3), 133–140.

Harrison, A. G., & De Jong, O. (2005). Exploring the use of multiple analogical models when teaching and learning chemical equilibrium. *Journal of Research in Science Teaching, 42*(10), 1135–1159.

Hattie, J.A.C. (1992). Measuring the effects of schooling. *Australian Journal of Education, 36*(1), 5–13.

Hattie, J.A.C. (2009). *Visible learning: A synthesis of over 800 meta-analyses relating to achievement.* New York: Routledge.

Hattie, J., & Timperley, H. (2007). The power of feedback. *Review of Educational Research, 77*(1), 81–112.

Hay, I., Elias, G., Fielding-Barnsley, R., Homel, R., & Freiberg, K. (2007). Language delays, reading delays, and learning difficulties. *Journal of Learning Disabilities, 40*, 400–409.

Henderlong, J., & Lepper, M. R. (2002). The effects of praise on children's intrinsic motivation: A review and synthesis. *Psychological Bulletin, 128*, 774–795.

Hidi, S., & Anderson, V. (1987). Providing written summaries: Task demands, cognitive operations, and implications for instruction. *Review of Educational Research, 56*, 473–493.

Hill, J. D., & Björk, C. L. (2008). *Classroom instruction that works with English language learners.* Alexandria, VA: ASCD.

Höffler, T. N., & Leutner, D. (2007). Instructional animation versus static pictures: A meta-analysis. *Learning and Instruction, 17*, 722–738.

Holyoak, K. J. (2005). Analogy. In K. J. Holyoak and R. G. Morrison (Eds.) *The Cambridge Handbook of Thinking and Reasoning* (pp. 117–142). New York: Cambridge University Press.

Hong, E., Milgram, R. M., & Rowell, L. L. (2004). Homework motivation and preference: A learner-centered homework approach. *Theory into Practice, 43*, 197–204.

Horner, S. L., & Gaither, S. M. (2004). Attributional retraining instruction with a second-grade class. *Early Childhood Education Journal, 31*(3), 165–170.

House, J. D. (2004). The effects of homework activities and teaching strategies for new mathematics topics on achievement of adolescent students in Japan: Results from the TIMSS 1999 assessment. *International Journal of Instructional Media, 31*(2), 199–210.

Howard, B. C. (1996, February). *A meta-analysis of scripted cooperative learning.* Paper presented at the annual meeting of the Eastern Educational Research Association, Boston, MA.

Hsu, Y.-S. (2008). Learning about seasons in a technologically enhanced environment: The impact of teacher-guided and student-centered instructional approaches on the process of students' conceptual change. *Science Education, 92*(2), 320–344.

Hubbell, E. (2009). *What's so different about literacy 2.0?* Retrieved from http://mcrel.typepad.com/mcrel_blog/2009/11/whats-so-different-about-literacy-20.html

Ingham, A. G., Levinger, G., Graves, J., & Peckham, V. (1974). The Ringelmann effect: Studies of group size and group performance. *Journal of Experimental Social Psychology, 10*(4), 371–384.

International Reading Association. (2010). Rope them in with hand gestures. *Reading Teacher, 64*(4), 282–284.

International Society for Technology in Education. (2007). National Educational Technology Standards for Students. Retrieved from http://www.iste.org/standards/nets-for-students/nets-student-standards-2007.aspx

Jensen, E. (2001). *Arts with the brain in mind.* Alexandria, VA: ASCD.

Jewitt, C. (2008). Multimodality and literacy in school classrooms. In J. Green, G. J. Kelly, and A. Luke (Eds.), *Review of research in education: Vol. 32. What counts as knowledge in educational settings: Disciplinary knowledge, assessment, and curriculum* (pp. 241–267). Thousand Oaks, CA: Sage.

Johnson, D. W. (1981). Student-student interaction: The neglected variable in education. *Educational Researcher, 10*(1), 5–10.

Johnson, D. W., & Johnson, F. P. (2009). *Joining together* (10th ed.). Upper Saddle River, NJ: Pearson.

Johnson, D. W., & Johnson, R. T. (1999). *Learning together and alone* (5th ed.). Boston, MA: Allyn & Bacon.

Johnson, D. W., & Johnson, R. T. (2003). Student motivation in co-operative groups. In R. M. Gillies & A. F. Ashman (Eds.), *Co-operative learning: The social and intellectual outcomes of learning in groups* (pp. 136–176). New York: Routledge Falmer.

Johnson, D. W., & Johnson, R. T. (2005). New developments in Social Interdependence Theory. *Genetic, Social, and General Psychological Monographs, 131*(4), 285–358.

Johnson, D. W., & Johnson, R. T. (2009). An educational psychology success story: Social interdependence theory and cooperative learning. *Educational Researcher, 38*(5), 365–379.

Kagan, S. (1985). *Cooperative learning resources for teachers.* Riverside, CA: University of California at Riverside.

Kagan, S. (1990). The structural approach to cooperative learning. *Educational Leadership, 47*(4), 12–15.

Kahle, A. L., & Kelly, M. L. (1994). Children's homework problems: A comparison of goal setting and parent training. *Behavior Therapy, 25*(2), 275–290.

Kamins, M. L., & Dweck, C. S. (1999). Person versus process praise and criticism: Implications for contingent self-worth and coping. *Developmental Psychology, 35*, 835–847.

Karpicke, J. D., & Roediger III, H. R. (2008). The critical importance of retrieval for learning. *Science, 319*, 966–968.

Kiewra, K. A. (1987). Note taking and review. The research and its implications. *Journal of Instructional Science, 16*, 233–249.

King, K., & Gurian, M. (2006). Teaching to the minds of boys. *Educational Leadership, 64*(1), 56–58, 60–61.

Knobel, M., & Wilber, D. (2009). Let's talk 2.0. *Educational Leadership, 66*(6), 20–24.

Kobayashi, K. (2006). Combined effects of note-taking/reviewing on learning and the enhancement through interventions: A meta-analytic review. *Educational Psychology, 26*, 459–477.

Kohn, A. (2006). *The homework myth.* Cambridge, MA: Da Capo Press.

Koutselini, M. (2009). Teacher misconceptions and understanding of cooperative learning: An intervention study. *Journal of Classroom Interaction, 43*(2), 34–44.

Kramarski, B., & Zeichner, O. (2001). Using technology to enhance mathematical reasoning: Effects of feedback and self-regulation learning. *Educational Media International, 38*(2/3), 77–82.

Kress, G. (1997). *Before writing: Rethinking the paths to literacy.* London: Routledge.

Lapp, D. (2004). *Teaching all the children: Strategies for developing literacy in an urban setting.* New York: Guilford Press.

Latane, B., Williams, K., & Harkins, S. G. (1979). Many hands make light work: The causes and consequences of social loafing. *Journal of Personality and Social Psychology, 37*(6), 822–832.

Lavoie, D. R. (1999). Effects of emphasizing hypothetico-predictive reasoning within the science learning cycle on high school students' process skills and conceptual understanding in biology. *Journal of Research in Science Teaching, 36*(10), 1127–1147.

Lavoie, D. R., & Good, R. (1988). The nature and use of prediction skills in biological computer simulation. *Journal of Research in Science Teaching, 25*(5), 334–360.

Lawson, A. E. (1988). A better way to teach biology. *The American Biology Teacher, 50*, 266–278.

Lefrancois, G. R. (1997). *Psychology for teaching* (9th ed.). Belmont, CA: Wadsworth.

Lehrer, R., & Chazen, D. (1998). *Designing learning environments for developing understanding of geometry and space.* Mahwah, NJ: Erlbaum.

Li, R., & Liu, M. (2007). Understanding the effects of databases as cognitive tools in a problem-based multimedia learning environment. *Journal of Interactive Learning Research 18*(3), 345–363.

Ling, L. M., Chik, P., & Pang, M. F. (2006). Patterns of variation in teaching the colour of light to Primary 3 students. *Instructional Science: An International Journal of Learning and Cognition, 34*(1), 1–19.

Lou, Y., Abrami, P. C., Spence, J. C., Paulsen, C., Chambers, B., & d'Apollonio, S. (1996). Within class grouping: A meta-analysis. *Review of Educational Research, 66*(4), 423–458.

Lucas, G. (2005, June 1). *Teaching "communication"* [Video file]. Retrieved from http://www.edutopia.org/george-lucas-teaching-communication-video

Madaus, G. F., & Stufflebeam, D. (Eds.). (1989). *Educational evaluation: Classic works of Ralph W. Tyler*. Boston: Kluwer Academic Press.

Makany, T., Kemp, J., & Dror, I. E. (2009). Optimising the use of note-taking as an external cognitive aid for increased learning. *British Journal of Educational Technology, 40*, 619–635.

Margolis, H., & McCabe, P. P. (2004). Self-efficacy: A key to improving the motivation of struggling learners. *Clearing House, 77*(6), 241–249.

Martorella, P. H. (1991). Knowledge and concept development in social studies. In J. P. Shaver (Ed.), *Handbook of research on social studies teaching and learning* (pp. 370–399). New York: McMillan.

Marx, R. W., Blumenfeld, P. C., Krajcik, J. S., Fishman, B., Soloway, E., Geier, R., & Tali Tal, R. (2004). Inquiry-based science in the middle grades: Assessment of learning in urban systemic reform. *Journal of Research in Science Teaching, 41*(10), 1063–1080.

Marzano, R. J., (1998). *A theory-based meta-analysis of research on instruction*. Aurora, CO: Mid-continent Research for Education and Learning.

Marzano, R. J., & Kendall, J. S. (1998). *Awash in a sea of standards*. Aurora, CO: Mid-continent Research for Education and Learning.

Marzano, R. J., & Pickering, D. J. (1997). *Dimensions of learning teacher's manual* (2nd ed.). Alexandria, VA: ASCD and Denver, CO: Mid-continent Research for Education and Learning.

Marzano, R. J., & Pickering, D. J. (2007). Special topic: The case for and against homework. *Educational Leadership, 64*(6), 74–79.

Marzano, R. J., Pickering, D. J., & Pollock, J. E. (2001). *Classroom instruction that works: Research-based strategies for increasing student achievement*. Alexandria, VA: ASCD.

Mathan, S. A., & Koedinger, K. R. (2002). An empirical assessment of comprehension fostering features in an intelligent tutoring system. In S. A. Cerri, G. Gouarderes, & F. Paraguacu (Eds.), *Intelligent Tutoring Systems, 6th International Conference, ITS2002* (Vol. 2363, pp. 330–343). New York: Springer Verlag.

Mathematical Sciences Education Board. (1990). *Reshaping school mathematics*. Washington, DC: National Academies Press.

Mbajiorgu, N. M., Ezechi, N. G., & Idoko, E. C. (2007). Addressing nonscientific presuppositions in genetics using a conceptual change strategy. *Science Education, 91*(3), 419–438.

McDaniel, M. A., Roediger, H. L., & McDermott, K. B. (2007). Generalizing test-enhanced learning from the laboratory to the classroom. *Psychonomic Bulletin & Review, 14*(2), 200–206.

McWhaw, K., Schnackenberg, H., Sclater, J., & Abrami, P. C. (2003). From co-operation to collaboration: Helping students become collaborative learners. In R. M. Gillies & A. F. Ashman (Eds.), *Co-operative learning: The social and intellectual outcomes of learning in groups* (pp. 69–86). New York: Routledge Falmer.

Medina, J. (2008). *Brain rules: 12 principals for surviving and thriving at work, home, and school*. Seattle, WA: Pear Press.

Mestre, J. P. (1994). Cognitive aspects of learning and teaching science. In S. J. Fitzimmons & L. C. Kerpelman (Eds.), *Teacher enhancements for elementary and secondary science and mathematics status, issues, and problems* (pp. 3.1–3.53). Arlington, VA: National Science Foundation.

Meyer, B.J.F., Middlemiss, W., Theodorou, E., Brezinski, K. L., & McDougall, J. (2002). Effects of structure strategy instruction delivered to fifth-grade children using the internet with and without the aid of older adult tutors. *Journal of Educational Psychology, 94*(3), 486–519.

Meyer, B.J.F., & Poon, L. W. (2001). Effects of structure strategy training and signaling on recall of text. *Journal of Educational Psychology, 93*, 141–159.

Michalchik, V., Rosenquist, A., Kozma, R., Kreikemeier, P., & Schank, P. (2008). Representational competence and chemical understanding in the high school chemistry classroom. In J. K. Gilbert, M. Reiner, and M. Nakhleh (Eds.), *Theory and practice in science education* (pp. 233–282). New York: Springer Verlag.

Miller, D., & Kelley, M. L. (1994). The use of goal setting and contingency contracting for improving children's homework performance. *Journal of Applied Behavior Analysis, 27*(1), 73–84.

Minotti, J. L. (2005). Effects of learning-style-based homework prescriptions on the achievement and attitudes of middle school students. *NASSP Bulletin, 89*, 67–89.

Mooney, P., Ryan, J. B., Uhing, B. M., Reid, R., & Epstein, M. H. (2005). A review of self-management interventions targeting academic outcomes for students with emotional and behavioral disorders. *Journal of Behavioral Education, 14*(3), 203–221.

Moore-Partin, T. C., Robertson, R. E., Maggin, D. M., Oliver, R. M., & Wehby, J. H. (2010). Using teacher praise and opportunities to respond to appropriate student behavior. *Preventing School Failure, 54*(3), 172–178.

Morgan, M. (1985). Self-monitoring of attained subgoals in private study. *Journal of Educational Psychology, 77*(6), 623–630.

Morgan, R. L., Whorton, J. E., & Gunsalus, C. (2000). A comparison of short-term and long-term retention: Lecture combined with discussion verses cooperative learning. *Journal of Instructional Psychology, 27*, 53–58.

National Council of Teachers of Mathematics. (2000). *Principles and standards for school mathematics*. Reston, VA: Author.

Newell, A., & Rosenbloom, P. S. (1981). Mechanisms of skill acquisition and the law of practice. In J. R. Anderson (Ed.), *Cognitive skills and their acquisition*. Hillsdale, NJ: Erlbaum.

Ogle, D.M. (1986). K-W-L: A teaching model that develops active reading of expository text. *Reading Teacher, 39*, 564–570.

Page-Voth, V., & Graham, S. (1999). Effects of goal setting and strategy use on the writing performance of students with writing and learning problems. *Journal of Educational Psychology, 91*(2), 230–240.

Paivio, A. (2006). Dual coding theory and education. Draft chapter for the conference on "Pathways to Literacy Achievement for High Poverty Children," The University of Michigan School of Education, September 29–October 1, 2006. Retrieved from http://readytolearnresearch.org/pathwaysconference/presentations/paivio.pdf

Palincsar, A. S., & Brown, A. L. (1985). Reciprocal teaching: Activities to promote reading with your mind. In T. L. Harris & E. J. Cooper (Eds.), *Reading, thinking and concept development: Strategies for the classroom*. New York: The College Board.

Pang, M.-F., & Marton, F. (2005). Learning theory as teaching resource: Enhancing students' understanding of economic concepts. *Instructional Science: An International Journal of Learning and Cognition, 33*(2), 159–191.

Partnership for 21st Century Skills. (n.d.) *Framework for 21st Century Learning*. Retrieved from http://p21.org

Pashler, H., Rohrer, D., Cepeda, N. J., & Carpenter, S. K. (2007). Enhancing learning and retarding forgetting: Choices and consequences. *Psychonomic Bulletin and Review, 14*(2), 187–193.

Patterson, K. B. (2005). Increasing positive outcomes for African American males in special education with the use of guided notes. *The Journal of Negro Education, 74*(4), 311–320.

Peterman, F. P. (Ed.). (2008). *Partnering to prepare urban teachers: A call to activism.* New York: Peter Lang.

Phan, H. P. (2009). Exploring students' reflective thinking practice, deep processing strategies, effort, and achievement goal orientations. *Educational Psychology, 29*(3), 297–313.

Pica, R. (2010). Linking literacy and movement. *Young Children, 65*(6), 72–73.

Pink, D. (2005). *A whole new mind: Why right-brainers will rule the future.* London: Penguin Books.

Pintrich, P. R., & Schrauben, B. (1992). Students' motivational beliefs and their cognitive engagement in classroom tasks. In D. Schunk & J. Meece (Eds.), *Student perceptions in the classroom: Causes and consequences* (pp. 149–183). Hillsdale, NJ: Lawrence Erlbaum.

Pintrich, P. R., & Schunk, D. H. (2002). *Motivation in education: Theory, research and applications* (2nd ed.). Upper Saddle River, NJ: Merrill Prentice Hall.

Piolat, A., Olive, T., & Kellogg, R. T. (2005). Cognitive effort during note taking. *Applied Cognitive Psychology, 19,* 291–312.

Pitler, H., & Hubbell, E. (2009). You can't judge a school by a classroom, or can you? *Changing Schools, 60,* 8–10.

Pitler, H., Hubbell, E. R., Kuhn, M., & Malenoski, K. (2007). *Using technology with classroom instruction that works.* Alexandria, VA: ASCD.

Plummer, J. (2009). Elementary students' development of astronomy concepts in the planetarium. *Journal of Research in Science Teaching, 46*(2), 192–209.

Prensky, M. (2001, October). Digital natives, digital immigrants. *On the Horizon, 9*(5). Retrieved from http://www.marcprensky.com

Reynolds, G. (2008). *Presentation zen: Simple ideas on presentation design and delivery.* Berkeley, CA: New Riders.

Richardson, A. (1983). Imagery: Definitions and types. In A. A. Sheikh (Ed.), *Imagery: Current theory, research, and application* (pp. 3–42). New York: Wiley.

Rivet, A. E., & Krajcik, J. S. (2004). Achieving standards in urban systemic reform: An example of a sixth grade project-based science curriculum. *Journal of Research in Science Teaching, 41*(7), 669–692.

Robinson, D. H., Katayama, A. D., Dubois, N. F., & Devaney, T. (1998). Interactive effects of graphic organizers and delayed review on concept acquisition. *The Journal of Experimental Education, 67,* 17–31.

Rohrer, D., & Taylor, K. (2007). The shuffling of mathematics practice problems boosts learning. *Instructional Science, 35,* 481–498.

Rohrer, D., Taylor, K., & Sholar, B. (2010). Tests enhance the transfer of learning. *Journal of Experimental Psychology, 36*(1), 233–239.

Romberg, T. A., & Carpenter, T. P. (1986). Research on teaching and learning mathematics: Two disciplines of scientific inquiry. In M. C. Wittrock (Ed.), *Handbook of research on teaching* (3rd ed.). New York: Macmillan.

Roseth, C. J., Johnson, D. W., & Johnson, R. T. (2008). Promoting early adolescents' achievement and peer relationships: The effects of cooperative, competitive, and individualistic goal structures. *Psychological Bulletin, 134*(2), 223–246.

Rule, A. C., & Furletti, C. (2004). Using form and function analogy object boxes to teach human body systems. *School Science and Mathematics 104*(4), 155–169.

Ryan, R. M., & Deci, E. L. (2000). Self-Determination Theory and the facilitation of intrinsic motivation, social development, and well-being. *American Psychologist, 55*(1), 68–78.

Sagor, R. (2000). *Guiding school improvement with action research*. Alexandria, VA: ASCD.

Sanders, W. L., & Horn, S. P. (1994). The Tennessee value-added assessment system (TVAAS): Mixed-model methodology in educational assessment. *Journal of Personnel Evaluation in Education, 8*, 299–311.

Scherer, M. (2007). Why focus on the whole child? *Educational Leadership, 64*(8), 7.

Schroeder, C. M., Scott, T. P., Tolson, H., Huang, T.-Y., & Lee, Y.-H. (2007). A meta-analysis of national research: Effects of teaching strategies on student achievement in science in the United States. *Journal of Research in Science Teaching, 44*(10), 1436–1460.

Schunk, D. H. (1999). Social-self interaction and achievement behavior. *Educational Psychologist, 34*(4), 219–227.

Schwartz, R., & Raphael, T. (1985). Concepts of definition: A key to improving students' vocabulary. *The Reading Teacher, 39*, 676–682.

Schwartz, N., Stroud, M., Hong, N., Lee, T., Scott, B., & McGee, S. (2006). Summoning prior knowledge: The influence of metaphorical priming on learning in a hypermedia environment. *Journal of Educational Computing Research, 35*(1), 1–30.

Sencibaugh, J. M. (2007). Meta-analysis of reading comprehension for students with learning disabilities: Strategies and implications. *Reading Improvement, 44*(1), 6–22.

Sharan, Y., & Sharan, S. (1992). *Expanding cooperative learning through group investigation*. New York: Teachers College Press.

Sheppard, J. A., & Taylor, K. M. (1999). Social loafing and expectancy-value theory. *Personality and Social Psychology Bulletin, 25*, 1147–1158.

Shirbagi, N. (2007). Feedback in formative evaluation and its effects on a sample of Iranian primary students' achievement in science. *Pedagogika, 88*, 99–105.

Shute, V. J. (2008). Focus on formative feedback. *Review of Educational Research, 78*(1), 153–189.

Sildus, T. I. (2006). The effect of a student video project on vocabulary retention of first-year secondary school German students. *Foreign Language Annals, 39*(1), 54–70.

Simons, K. D., & Klein, J. D. (2007). The impact of scaffolding and student achievement levels in a problem-based learning environment. *Instructional Science: An International Journal of the Learning Sciences, 35*(1), 41–72.

Simonson, B., Fairbanks, S., Briesch, A., Myers, D., & Sugai, G. (2008). Evidence-based practices in classroom management: Considerations for research to practice. *Education and Treatment of Children, 31*(3), 351–380.

Slavin, R. E. (1978). Student teams and achievement divisions. *Journal of Research and Development in Education, 12*, 39–49.

Slavin, R. E. (1983). *Cooperative Learning*. New York: Longman.

Slavin, R. E. (1990). *Cooperative learning: Theory, research, and practice*. Boston: Allyn & Bacon.

Souvignier, E., & Kronenberger, J. (2007). Cooperative learning in third graders' jigsaw groups for mathematics and science with and without questioning training. *The British Psychological Society, 77*, 755–771.

Stiggins, R. J. (2001). *Student-involved classroom assessment* (3rd ed.). Upper Saddle River, NJ: Prentice-Hall.

Stiggins, R. J., Arter, J. A., Chappuis, J., & Chappuis, S. (2006). *Classroom assessment for student learning: Doing it right–using it well*. Portland, OR: Educational Testing Service.

Stone, B., & Urquhart, V. (2008). *Remove limits to learning with systematic vocabulary instruction*. Denver, CO: Mid-continent Research for Education and Learning.

Taba, H. (1962). *Curriculum development: Theory and practice*. New York: Harcourt, Brace, and World.

Takala, M. (2006). The effects of reciprocal teaching on reading comprehension in mainstream and special (SLI) education. *Scandinavian Journal of Educational Research, 50*(5), 559–576.

Tarhan, L., & Acar, B. (2007). Problem-based learning in an eleventh grade chemistry class: 'Factors affecting cell potential.' *Research in Science and Technology Education, 25*(3), 351–369.

Tomlinson, C. A. (1995). *How to differentiate instruction in mixed ability classrooms*. Alexandria, VA: ASCD.

Tomlinson, C. A. (2001). *How to differentiate instruction in mixed ability classrooms* (2nd ed.). Alexandria, VA: ASCD.

Tomlinson, C. A. (2004). *Fulfilling the promise of the differentiated classroom: Strategies and tools for responsive teaching*. Alexandria, VA: ASCD.

Tweed, A. (2009). *Designing effective science instruction: What works in science classrooms*. Arlington, VA.: National Science Teachers Association.

Urdan, T. (2004). Using multiple methods to assess students' perceptions of classroom goal structures. *European Psychologist, 9*(4), 222–231.

Valle, A., & Callanan, M. A. (2006). Similarity comparisons and relational analogies in parent-child conversations about science topics. *Merrill-Palmer Quarterly, 52*(1), 96–124.

Vatterott, C. (2009). *Rethinking homework: Best practices that support diverse needs*. Alexandria, VA: ASCD.

Vygotsky, L. S. (1978). *Mind in society: The development of higher psychological processes*. Cambridge, MA: Harvard University Press.

Wagner, P., Schober, B., & Spiel, C. (2008). Time investment and time management: An analysis of time students spend working at home for school. *Educational Research and Evaluation, 14*(2), 139–153.

Walberg, H. J. (1999). Productive teaching. In H. C. Waxman & H. J. Walberg (Eds.), *New directions for teaching practice and research* (pp. 75–104). Berkeley, CA: McCutchen Publishing Corporation.

Walker, B. (2003). The cultivation of student self-efficacy in reading and writing. *Reading and Writing Quarterly: Overcoming Learning Difficulties, 19*(2), 173–187.

Walker, C.O., Greene, B. A., & Mansell, R. A. (2006). Identification with academics, intrinsic/extrinsic motivation, and self-efficacy as predictors of cognitive engagement. *Learning and Individual Differences, 16*, 1–12.

Walton, P. D., & Walton, L. M. (2002). Beginning reading by teaching in rime analogy: Effects on phonological skills, letter-sound knowledge, working memory, and word-reading strategies. *Scientific Studies of Reading, 6*(1), 79–115.

Ward, J. D., & Lee, C. L. (2004). Teaching strategies for FCS: Student achievement in problem-based learning versus lecture-based instruction. *Journal of Family and Consumer Sciences, 96*(1), 73–76.

Warton, P. M. (2001). The forgotten voices in homework: Views of the students. *Educational Psychologist, 36*(3), 155–165.

Waters, J. T., Marzano, R. J., & McNulty, B. A. (2003). *Balanced leadership: What 30 years of research tells us about the effect of leadership on student achievement*. Aurora, CO: Mid-continent Research for Education and Learning.

Weiss, I., Kramarski, B., & Talis, S. (2006). Effects of multimedia environments on kindergarten children's mathematical achievements and style of learning. *Educational Media International, 43*(1), 3–17.

White, K., Hohn, R., & Tollefson, N. (1997). Encouraging elementary students to set realistic goals. *Journal of Research in Childhood Education, 12*, 48–57.

White, R. T., & Tisher, R. P. (1986). Research on natural sciences. In M. C. Wittrock (Ed.), *Handbook of research on teaching* (pp. 874–905). New York: McMillan.

Wigfield, A., & Eccles, J. (2000). Expectancy-value theory of achievement motivation. *Contemporary Educational Psychology, 25*, 68–81.

Wittrock, M. C., & Alesandrini, K. (1990). Generation of summaries and analogies and analytic and holistic abilities. *American Educational Research Journal, 27*(3), 489–502.

Woolfolk, A. (2004). *Educational Psychology.* Boston: Pearson.

Wright, S. P., Horn, S. P., & Sanders, W. L. (1997). Teacher and classroom context effects on student achievement: Implications for teacher evaluation. *Journal of Personnel Evaluation in Education, 11,* 57–67.

Zimmerman, B. J. (2000). Self-efficacy: An essential motive to learn. *Contemporary Educational Psychology, 25,* 82–91.

# Index

The letter *f* following a page number denotes a figure.

# About the Authors

**Ceri B. Dean** is vice president for field services at Mid-continent Research for Education and Learning (McREL). She is responsible for the development and successful implementation of McREL's professional development, technical assistance, and consultation services. She has served as the director of large-scale projects, including the North Central Comprehensive Center at McREL, a U.S. Department of Education–funded technical assistance center. She is codeveloper of materials to facilitate delivery of McREL's comprehensive approach to school improvement, Success in Sight, and she has coauthored a number of McREL publications. She is a former high school mathematics teacher and holds a Ph.D. in Curriculum and Instruction from the University of Connecticut at Storrs and an M.S. in Atmospheric Science from Colorado State University.

**Elizabeth Ross Hubbell** is a principal consultant at McREL. She conducts workshops and training for K–12 teachers on research-based instructional strategies and technology integration, writes curriculum models for online classes, conducts technology audits for districts, and trains school and district leaders in using Power Walkthrough software. She holds an M.A. in Information and Learning Technologies from the University of Colorado–Denver and a B.S. in Early Childhood/Elementary Education from the University of Georgia. Elizabeth was one of four national finalists in Technology & Learning's Ed Tech Leader of the Year 2003. She is coauthor of *Using Technology with Classroom Instruction that Works* and *The Future of Schooling: Educating America in 2020*.

**Howard Pitler** is a senior director at McREL. He conducts workshops and training for K–12 teachers on research-based instructional strategies and technology integration, conducts technology audits for districts, and works with school and district leaders in using Power Walkthrough classroom observation software. He holds an Ed.D. in Educational Administration from Wichita State University, an M.A. in Music Performance from Wichita State, and a B.A. in Music Education from Indiana State University. Howard is an Apple Distinguished Educator and a Smithsonian Laureate, and he was a 1997 National Distinguished Principal. He has been published in several journals, and he is coauthor of *Using Technology with Classroom Instruction that Works*.

**Bj Stone** is a principal consultant at McREL. She facilitates learning sessions with teachers and administrators in the areas of research-based instructional strategies, vocabulary instruction, curriculum development, and assessment design. Bj was designated as a Teaching Fellow in a large National Science Foundation–funded grant for preservice teachers and has been published in the *Journal of Teacher Education*. Bj is a former middle and high school science teacher, university instructor, and assistant superintendent. She has a B.S in Biology, a M.S. in Science Education, and an Ed.D. in Educational Leadership and Policy Study from the University of Northern Colorado.

## About McREL

Mid-continent Research for Education and Learning (McREL) is a nationally recognized, nonprofit education research and development organization, headquartered in Denver, Colorado with offices in Honolulu, Hawai'i and Omaha, Nebraska. Since 1966, McREL has helped translate research and professional wisdom about what works in education into practical guidance for educators. Our 120-plus staff members and affiliates include respected researchers, experienced consultants, and published writers who provide educators with research-based guidance, consultation, and professional development for improving student outcomes.